.hack//G.U.™

VOL_01 : THE TERROR OF DEATH

STORY BY
TATSUYA HAMAZAKI

ILLUSTRATED BY
YUZUKA MORITA

LIGHT NOVELS

A  Prose Novel

TOKYOPOP Inc.
5900 Wilshire Boulevard, Suite 2000
Los Angeles, CA 90036
www.TOKYOPOP.com

STORY	Tatsuya Hamazaki
ILLUSTRATIONS	Yuzuka Morita
TRANSLATION	Gemma Collinge
DESIGN AND LAYOUT	Erika Terriquez
FAN CONSULTANTS	Christopher Wagner and Colin Farrell
SENIOR EDITOR	Jenna Winterberg
PRE-PRODUCTION SUPERVISOR	Vincente Rivera, Jr.
PRE-PRODUCTION SPECIALIST	Lucas Rivera
MANAGING EDITOR	Vy Nguyen
SENIOR DESIGNER	Louis Csontos
SENIOR DESIGNER	James Lee
SENIOR EDITOR	Bryce P. Coleman
SENIOR EDITOR	Jenna Winterberg
ASSOCIATE PUBLISHER	Marco F. Pavia
PRESIDENT AND C.O.O.	John Parker
C.E.O. & CHIEF CREATIVE OFFICER	Stu Levy

First TOKYOPOP printing: February 2009

10 9 8 7 6 5 4 3 2 1

Printed in the USA

.hack // G.U. Vol. 1 SHI NO KYOFU
© Tatsuya HAMAZAKI 2007
First published in Japan in 2007 by KADOKAWA SHOTEN
PUBLISHING CO., LTD., Tokyo.
English Translation rights arranged with KADOKAWA
SHOTEN PUBLISHING CO., LTD. Tokyo through TUTTLE-
MORI AGENCY, INC., Tokyo.
English text © 2009 TOKYOPOP Inc.

Library of Congress Cataloging-in-Publication Data

Hamazaki, Tatsuya.
  [Shi no kyofu. English]
  Terror of Death / Tatsuya Hamazaki ; [illustration, Yuzuka
Morita ; translation, Gemma Collinge].
    p. cm. -- (.hack//G.U. ; 1)
  "First published in Japan in 2007 by Kadokawa Publishing
Co. . . . Tokyo"--T.p. verso.
  ISBN 978-1-4278-1381-7
  I. Morita, Yuzuka. II. Collinge, Gemma. III. Title.
  PL871.A53S45 2008010a 2008045213
  895.6'36--dc22   2008045213

DEFINITION

PK [Player Killer / Killing]
The act of attacking and killing other player characters (PCs) in a massively multiplayer online role-playing game (MMORPG). Also refers to players who perform such acts. Although some PK in order to steal gold and items, others treat the role of a PK as a play style, depicting the role of a murderer within the game.

PKK [Player-Killer Killer / Killing]
To Player Kill a PK. Also refers to players who habitually perform this act.

Contents

Prologue ● 007

Chapter_01: Tri-Edge ● 010

Chapter_02: Raven ● 043

Chapter_03: Possession ● 070

Chapter_04: Demon Palace ● 097

Chapter_05: Emptiness ● 136

Chapter_06: The Royal Island ● 173

Afterword ● 194

PROLOGUE

A girl laid on the pure white bed, her cheeks sunken, her arm muscles atrophied, her hair slick with grease and as hard as a cheap wig. Her breathing was shallow, and murky veins bubbled up visibly beneath her dried, ashen skin.

She was ash gray. The color of death.

Ryou Misaki was visiting Shino Nanao in her room at University Hospital.

The medical machinery that monitored her pulse and heart rate indicated levels at which the maintenance of human life should not have been possible. Yet Shino was still alive—in a place outside all common sense, in that space between this and the distant shore, like a sleeping beauty, frozen in time by some terrible spell.

"You're a good friend," a nurse said as she entered the room. "I mean, coming here every other day."

The young nurse surely was simply trying to offer Ryou some support.

"I live nearby," Ryou said, side-stepping further explantion in an attempt to avoid more questions about his personal life.

"I can't believe she's been like this for half a year."

"You still have no idea what the cause is?" Ryou worked hard to keep his voice level as he asked the question. He was grateful to the attentive nurse, but he didn't want to become overly familiar with her.

"The doctors are doing everything they can, but . . ." She shook her head.

Shino Nanao had been in an unexplained coma for the last six months.

The cause was still unknown. All that the doctors could do—all that *anyone* could do—was attach tubes to facilitate her bodily functions and nutritional needs, simply keeping her alive. They couldn't save her.

No matter how hard Ryou wished to hear it, Shino's voice was lost to him.

Shino's shining smile had been snatched away from *both* Ryou's worlds, from the real world—

"She fell unconscious while playing that game, right? 'The World'?"

—and from the 'net, too. That was the lead in to all the mysteries now surrounding Shino.

Shino Nanao had fallen into her coma *while playing an online game*.

"Who brought those flowers?" Ryou asked the nurse. A vase of gerbera daisies had been placed in the room.

"You didn't bring them?" The nurse tilted her head, puzzled, before leaving the room.

Ryou touched the flowers.

Shino was just like these daisies now, cut off from the real world, the earth in which she'd grown her roots.

He stroked the silky, moist petals. Pollen stained his fingers. When he licked his fingertips, the taste was sweet, bitter. The smell was like of someone else.

I'm . . .

He desperately sought an answer in the destroyed, corpselike body and mind before him. In the depths of his sadness, anger, pain, and despair, Ryou found the one he needed to tell—and there, in the sickness like mud, Ryou made a vow.

"I'm going to save you!"

The cicadas started to chirp outside the window. One . . . then two, three. Like flies drawn by the stench of death in the hospital room, they attached themselves to the wall outside the window, vocally protesting the shortness of life.

I'm going to get it back. All of it.

CHAPTER_01 : TRI-EDGE

ONE

The sound of the wind passed from Ryou's right ear across to his left. A merciless sun flamed down from the cracked sky above. There was no sign of life on the dried-out, wild plain. And everything in the scene that spoke to human feeling was transmitted through a sunglasslike M2D display.

There was no heat. So it was hot, but . . .

The intent of the players, each gripping his or her own controller, was reflected violently, vividly.

"Help!"

Screams periodically overwrote the stream of abuse.

Out on the field, a party of three was surrounded by a group of more than twenty opponents. There were no monsters present—both parties comprised Player Characters. A nasty bunch of seasoned veterans were picking on a group of close friends, beginners—that was the scene now unfolding. Two of the beginners already had been taken out, reduced to pathetic ash gray corpses.

Death.

There were many styles of play within the online game The World. Some players even went as far as to stake their (digital) lives.

"Ha! A pack of newbie losers."

A husky female voice rang out, and a Blade Brandier equipped with a sword like a length of thorny bramble stepped forward.

Her hair was curly and red, and she wore a brazen leather costume that exposed her navel. Patterns were painted here and there across her lightly tanned skin. It was a character design of someone who'd chosen to play the bad guy. She was apparently the leader of this group.

"YOU'RE HORRIBLE!"
"WHY WOULD YOU DO SOMETHING LIKE THIS?"
"PLEASE, STOP IT!"

The voiceless log in the message window was filled with complaints from the beginners who had already been killed. Only here was such a spectacle possible—the dead talking back to those who'd killed them.

"Why are you killing other players?!"

A Harvest Cleric, one of those who had just lost most of her companions, directed the voice of a young girl at the female Blade Brandier.

"Why? You aren't simply hurting unfeeling characters within a game! Why can't you see that you're also hurting the feelings of other players?" The Harvest Cleric spoke firmly.

She was right. In all likelihood, she was right.

But in the harsh, impersonal online world, attempting this kind of reasoning with Player Killers was pure folly. Here in The World, people played because they could ignore reality and all its constraints, making morals as worthless as a cheap knife. Here, there were only the rules—no right or wrong. If you wanted to prove your existence here in this sea of data, you simply had to prove you were strong.

"LOL."

"Ha ha ha ha ha ha ha" . . . scornful laughter came across the voice chat. *It's better to kill than be killed,* it seemed to say. And when faced with the evil of humanity totally exposed—something rarely confronted in the real world—the female Harvest Cleric lost her voice. The feelings of the player controlling the PC avatar were obviously in tatters. Her naïve, pure heart had been trampled into the dirt. A girl will cry when her treasured doll is broken, after all. Those tears alone were motivation enough for many of the online Player Killers.

"Words, words, pointless words . . . Strength is everything in The World." The female Blade Brandier flicked back her flaming hair and poked at the Harvest Cleric with the tip of her bramble sword.

"Aaah!"

"The weak are there to be hunted! In the real world and in this World!"

But just as the female Blade Brandier was about to deliver the final blow, a black shadow crept up along some overhanging rocks. And that black shadow, which had seen everything, now descended.

Exhaust roared.

The shadow lowered itself like a bird of prey plunging down from above, directly mowing down one among the group of PKs. A smaller shadow separated itself from the billowing steam bike, jumping clear and pulling his twin swords out in mid-air before plunging them into the fallen PK.

"Grein?!"

Seeing one of her minions, a male Edge Punisher with the body of a sumo wrestler, crumble to the ground, the female Blade Brandier took a step back. The PKs switched their target from the girl Harvest Cleric, their M2Ds tracking this chaos-spreading newcomer.

An Adept Rogue dressed all in black . . .

"Bordeaux! It's that guy we've been hearing about!"

"What?!" the female Blade Brandier shouted back at another of her men, a Twin Blade with a top-knot hairstyle.

He flicked his controller. The black Adept Rogue in the center of his M2D—the Player Character controlled by Ryou Misaki—responded to the movement, putting his twin swords away and drawing a huge chainsword that now appeared on his back.

"You're gonna get—"

But the Adept Rogue sliced top-knot clean in two without even letting him finish his insult.

He turned ash gray. The color of death.

Though the man had just been sliced in two by a massive chainsaw, there was no terrible death scream, no fountain of blood as one might expect from some gory horror flick. He simply collapsed to the ground, transformed into an ash gray corpse.

The World was a game aimed at all ages, from the very young to the very old. And yet there was no limitation on the types of exchanges that took place within it. This World was warped. This World could be a terrible place.

"Negimaru?!" Bordeaux shouted the name of her fallen comrade, flinching back again. The damage caused was an indication of the difference in level between her and their attacker, and that difference was enough to more than fill her cup with despair. Furthermore, the black Adept Rogue, Haseo, had his own special name among PKs. . . .

"The Terror of Death . . . Haseo, the PKK!" Bordeaux shouted again. But before she even had time to ready her weapon, the black Adept Rogue was suddenly standing behind her.

He was nothing less than a black demon.

His base character model was a silver-haired youth. However, the only part that could still be called humanlike was above the neck. His body was a writhing mess of twisted curses. Plated in living armor that was covered with sharp, jutting spikes and that had a long tail hanging behind it, Haseo looked like nothing less than the rebirth of the ancient sword-and-armor dragons. He had completely maxed out the third form of the Adept Rogue, which allowed him

to use three types of weapons and placed him within the top five percent of players above level 100. Such a monster could only be created by a real 'net junkie, one who had totally given up life in the real world and poured his all into The World.

"Tell me what you know about Tri-Edge." The voice of Ryou Misaki passed through the microphone on his MD2 and radiated out into The World as the voice of his PC, Haseo.

"Huh?"

"The PK." His speech was picked up by voice recognition software that ran at ninety-eight percent accuracy; then, it was converted into text, which appeared in the message window. "Those killed by him are apparently unable to return to the game. Ever."

Haseo placed the blade of his huge scythe against Bordeaux's neck. Haseo was an Adept Rogue who used twin swords, a great sword, and a scythe.

"Tri-Edge?" Bordeaux sounded for a moment as though the name meant something to her. "Don't go believing all the trash you read on the boards, loser!"

She spun and swung her thorn blade, but the Adept Rogue was no longer in its path. Even as Bordeaux processed her surprise, Haseo's scythe sliced through the air and claimed her life.

Death dyed her red locks gray.

"Worthless!" Ryou spat, hardly glancing at Bordeaux's body.

The remaining PKs scattered like baby spiders running for cover. PKs always gave up easily, never fought to the last. They knew that trying to resist an undefeatable enemy was merely a waste of healing items. So in the face of obvious defeat, they would simply give up their lives.

DON'T THINK YOU CAN JUST KILL THE MIGHTY BORDEAUX AND GET AWAY WITH IT!

Leaving a voiceless throwaway line behind, Bordeaux's gray corpse vanished. She had logged out.

"You killed them?"

It might be called "killing," but this wasn't real death.

When Bordeaux logged in again, she would face an experience point penalty, and then she'd get right back to PKing as though nothing had happened. That was all. There was no value, no meaning in this fake death.

But Shino . . .

"Excuse me . . ."

Ryou turned when he heard the voice, reactively targeting the speaker, Haseo adopting a fighting stance.

His new target didn't react to Haseo's movements, though. She simply stood there.

One of the victims of the PK attack, she was dressed in a clean, neat lace costume that had small bird-wing accessories on the shoulders. Haseo could've snapped her slender form like a toothpick, if he so choose. She was merely a young Harvest Cleric.

Ryou's breath caught. The face of the girl on his display . . .

"Shino?"

"Excuse me?" The puzzled, "who are you talking to?" look on the Cleric's face quickly brought Ryou back to himself.

With a loud, deliberate click of his tongue, Haseo climbed back on his steam bike and departed in a roar of exhaust.

TWO

That day . . . six months ago . . . It was winter, and a cold wind had been blowing.

The meeting place was a coffee shop in front of Ikebukuro station. Having placed his order from the menu, Ryou used the wallet function on his cell phone to pay. The e-money chime rang out, and he was given a receipt with a number on it. "One short hot mocha coming right up," said the part-timer behind the counter. She hurriedly poured out a shot of freshly brewed espresso.

"Number 28, your order is ready."

Taking his drink, he moved to an empty seat.

Beyond the glass partition, the smokers drowned in wreaths of their own smoke, which filled their small allotted space. They were like animals in a zoo.

Ryou glanced at the PDA of an office worker sitting next to him. *"Construction on Central Linear Bullet Train to Begin."* Half a century had passed since the start of plans for a linear motor car to run between Tokyo and Osaka in only one hour, and now it was finally going to be built. Construction costs were estimated at fifteen trillion yen. Shinjuku station in Tokyo would have a super-deep underground station added, at a depth of more than one hundred thirty feet. Everything was scheduled to be completed in ten years time, by 2027, at which point Ryou would be twenty-seven.

He looked at himself in a mirror on a nearby pillar, adjusting his ash-colored hair. His scalp still stung from the first bleaching of his life the day before. He'd taken pointers from a fashion magazine to style it. He'd also taken a bath that morning, brushed his teeth, smoothed his eyebrows, sprayed his underarms, and made sure his breath was fresh.

"Are you . . . Ryou Misaki?"

When he heard his name being spoken, Ryou leapt up from his seat as though he'd been kicked in the shin.

"Ah . . . uh . . ."

A living nightmare. He had stumbled right off the blocks.

She was wearing short boots, a pleated denim skirt, and a black knit top with a fur vest. A well-used canvas tote bag was slung over her shoulder. She was casually dressed. He suddenly lamented his persistent desire to be liked—or at least, not to be disliked—a desire that had driven him into the most expensive store he could find, into clothes that didn't suit him and pointed, uncomfortable shoes, all on the recommendation of the shop assistant. A crushing weight of shame pushed him down into a blinding, cloying mud. He'd practiced his opening speech so much, and yet now the words were stuck uselessly in his throat. The more he panicked, the more it was like pushing the accelerator and brake at the same time—jarring, stuttering, grinding to a halt.

His gaze swam somewhere around her shoulders. She was thin, and totally different from the people he normally hung around with. Different clothes . . . a different gender. He breathed in the scent of a woman. She had said in her mail that she was college student.

Ryou tried again to look into the eyes of the girl in front of him . . . and was plunged into despair again by his lack of ability to speak. He felt as though his breathing was about to cut off, but he finally managed to utter her name, with an intonation as though he were asking for something.

"Shino?"

"Shino Nanao, that's me." That was her self-introduction.

Ryou had told her his full real name but had failed to get all of hers.

"Ah, the same name as your PC?"

"Unlike you, huh? Haseo isn't Haseo out here, is he?" She smiled happily.

Someone listening in surely would have no idea what they were talking about. But the exchange served to instantly bring them much closer together.

"Weren't you going to . . . mail me once you got here?" Ryou almost immediately slipped into his habitual hesitant voice chat, though he tried to correct it as he asked the question.

"Once I got here, I kinda just guessed who you were."

She, Shino Nanao, smiled wildly, obviously trying to put him at ease. That was how stiff and frozen Ryou must have looked.

The two of them had never met, but they'd been friends for almost two months now—not in the real world, but online, in the largest MMORPG in the world, The World.

In this virtual world, they had interacted as their respective PCs, Haseo and Shino. Their relationship now was supposed to spread out into the real world. Ryou had been planning on confessing himself to her, telling her that he loved her. Telling Shino. Telling the leg-tremblingly beautiful girl in front of him, the *real* Shino . . .

But that was the last time Ryou ever spoke to her.

● ◆ ●

In 2005, the First Network Crisis—triggered by the virus called Pluto's Kiss—brought the 'net society of that time to an end. All the OS and security software was corrupted . . . destroyed. The virus wreaked damage on a biblical scale to global finances, plunging the world into the so-called 'Net Dark Ages, in which almost all walks of life were kicked back twenty years.

After more than two years of stagnation, the day of the Maiden's Kiss came: On December 14, 2007, the 'net reopened for public access, along with the absolute ALTIMIT OS. The MMORPG The World also started service on this day, eventually becoming the largest online game in the world, with more than twenty million users. Cyber Connect Corporation, which developed and maintained The World and had strong links with ALTIMIT Ltd. (exclusive rights holders of the core software of the new Internet age), now stepped onto the world stage as the new leader in the provision of entertainment content.

Then, at the end of 2015, Cyber Connect Corporation released The World R:2, the official sequel to the game that was still the flagship for online gaming. Due to market saturation after the game's original release, the number of users had fallen to less than twelve million by that point, but this new version was no less well received because of that.

Summer 2017. A quarter century since the birth of the MMORPG, The World R:2 was continually updating and remained in the center of a whirl of praise, criticism . . . and unbelievable popularity.

Δ SERVER ROOT TOWN: THE ETERNAL CITY OF MAC ANU

The World's Japanese servers were divided up into a number of smaller servers, and each designated a recommended level along with a Root Town named after a letter of the Greek alphabet. The Δ Server, for beginner players, was linked to here, in the town of Mac Anu.

As suggested by its alias, "The Eternal City," Mac Anu also appeared in The World's original version. With canals cutting through its stone paved streets, the section called Old Town was reminiscent of Venice in the real world. Beyond its waterways loomed the steel high-rises of New Town, erected there by the new culture of steam. New Town, however, was simply a distant background—players could not travel there. Within The World, a couple of thousand years had passed since the original game. Now a faction known as Arvakv the Innovators was making this place their base of operations.

Those were the game settings.

● ⬡ ●

The Adept Rogue, decked out in black, crossed the bridge that connected the gate with the city, the canal beneath shimmering with the evening sun's rays.

"Anyone selling twin swords?"

"Health Drinks, cheaper than in the shops!"

"Looking for one Harvest Cleric around level 20. Plenty of experience!"

The fountain square in the central ward of Mac Anu was a natural gathering place for players. Their chat filled his ears, the log in the message window scrolling smoothly downward. A Root Town was a great place to find all sorts of financial activities. The town had the traditional facilities you would find in an RPG, including a weapon shop and an armor shop, but more than half of the transactions within The World took place between players. Anyone in a Root Town could trade with other players or open his own shop. The player prices were generally cheaper than official shop costs, and if you had the GP, you could obtain even rare items. Many players enjoyed the traders' life, both obtaining and selling items. There were as many play styles as there were players in The World. That was freedom—or at least, that was lack of regulation. Players also used the Root Town to gather quest parties before heading out into the adventure areas.

However, the world view, conversation, deals, companions . . . Ryou rejected all these forms of communication, indeed rejecting the very fact that The World was a game. And yet, that was still where he could be found. Ryou had to remain in The World, remain as Haseo, because . . .

"Your PC is like murder given flesh, Haseo . . . The Terror of Death."

As Haseo passed in front of the fountain, he found another PC standing in front of him, a young male Blade Brandier. His long hair was tied back, and he had dark circles around his narrow eyes, along with samurai-style armor that made him look like something from a period movie.

Ryou formed Haseo's third form into a cruel smile, repelling the look this newcomer gave him with a wall of silence.

"PCs who kill other PCs . . . I deplore the infestation of PKing here in The World"—Ryou targeted the Blade Brandier in the samurai armor even as the other player started his speech; the name of his PC was displayed: Sakaki—"but does that mean those like you are in the right? Those PKKs who seek to resolve this problem with force?"

"How would I know?" Ryou replied.

"Why do you add more links to the chain of hatred? I, Sakaki of Moon Tree Guild, find that I cannot easily overlook this!" The PC called Sakaki invoked the name of the guild he belonged to.

Guilds within The World were organized groups of players. They ranged from those with just a few members to those with a couple of thousand, and were created for a multitude of reasons— to gather others to chat with, to help in creation of rare weapons, to form groups of traders in the truest sense of the word "guild," or simply to concentrate on PKing.

Among these guilds, Moon Tree was one of the largest, and its name frequently appeared on board posts. For example, complaints were posted that it was some sort of dangerous religious cult, its members putting on airs as keepers of the peace although they were not official CC Corp Game Masters.

"Sorry. I have all the friends I need." Haseo attempted to walk off, treating Sakaki as nothing more than one of those annoying canvassers who hung around outside train stations, but a young girl spoke up.

"It's only polite to listen to everything someone has to say, you know."

Ryou swallowed hard when he saw the face on his display . . . it was the Harvest Cleric who had been under attack from the PKs.

"That's simply good manners." The girl gave him a cheerful smile. Inputting emotion commands allowed PCs within The World to perform a range of fixed emotional expressions, spanning from joy to sadness. Just another of the communication tools the software offered.

"Have I upset you?" Haseo's lengthy stare obviously was making the girl uncomfortable.

"You said he mistook you for someone else, right, Atoli?"

Atoli . . . She wasn't Shino. She was Atoli. Ryou silently repeated the name.

Sakaki cut in. "That's right. It's not uncommon to meet two PCs who use the same model in an online game."

Sakaki's character model gave a wry laugh.

When starting out in The World, each player used the character edit system to alter the height, body shape, face, hairstyle, skin color, costume, and other elements to create his own unique PC. There were a large number of parts available, offering almost limitless combinations, but there were obvious trends in the tastes of players, and it wasn't uncommon to bump into a PC who looked oddly familiar.

Sakaki had thus come to the realization that Ryou must have mistaken Atoli for a PC with a similar design, which was exactly the case.

The girl Harvest Cleric was *exactly the same* as Shino, aside from her coloring. Shino had silver hair and black clothing. Atoli, standing in front of him now, had blonde hair and green clothing. This was a minor distinction, something that the display itself could be used to compensate for if he so desired. It meant nothing when framed in his sepia memories, memories that had been cut short just six months ago. Shino, who he could now only meet in his memories . . . the PC of Shino Nanao was now overlaid with the girl called Atoli, the girl in front of him.

A chime rang out indolently, and Haseo's attention was dragged back to his display.

It was a personal chat—a one-on-one message that reached only the PC it was specifically directed to. There were numerous chat modes, including party chat (messages sent only to party members) and guild chat (messages sent only to members of the same guild). Chat during an online game gave every player ESP.

HASEO.

Only Haseo—rather, his player, Ryou—could see the message log for the personal chat.

HE'S GOING TO APPEAR TODAY. YOU KNOW THE PLACE.

The message was from . . . *Ovan?* Ryou's eyes narrowed at the sender's name. That took him back a bit, a name he hadn't seen in his message window for half a year.

Ryou, shaken, operated his controls to swing Haseo's view around the player-filled square. Ovan wasn't there . . . there was no sign of the PC who had contacted Haseo.

"I know the place?" Ryou whispered. And then he suddenly worked it out and started Haseo off running.

"Hey! Where do you think you're going?" The other PCs must have thought he was running away.

Sakaki, obviously unaware that Haseo had received a personal message, shouted behind him: "You may think of yourself as dealing justice, but you PKKs are no different than PKs."

So, the rumors were true. Ryou gave a wry laugh. That was the kind of talk Moon Tree Guild was famous for. Justice? Such seemingly irrelevant words were the only way Haseo could regulate his continued existence in The World. He couldn't comprehend others. They were ignorant, and they didn't care about others, simply blaming and lecturing them for the sake of their own self-gratification.

"PK, PKK, they're both the same. They both hurt others." Even Atoli, the female Harvest Cleric who'd been saved as a result of Haseo's actions before, now spoke out against him. Self-righteous indeed.

She definitely, definitely wasn't Shino. Shino would have understood what Haseo was doing.

"You're right." Haseo's initial reply made it sound as though he'd understood Atoli's words, and she smiled again.

"PK just achieves an in-game death, that's all."

"Huh?"

"What I'm looking for is real death." With that comment, Haseo was gone, leaving only the roar of his steam engines behind.

Atoli's smile turned to vinegar.

As if he would tell people like that why he'd become a PKK.

"He's crazy." That was Sakaki's dismissal. Atoli, too, with her face like Shino's, didn't chase after Haseo.

● ⬡ ●

THREE

Each Root Town had a teleportation device called a Chaos Gate, from which players could head out into the adventure areas. The World system allowed players to travel to any desired area from the Root Town through a combination of three keywords or phrases, automatically creating areas based upon those word combinations. For example, inputting the three words "Beautiful," "Leading," and "Journey" would create the area "Beautiful Leading Journey." The number of these combinations was virtually infinite, making it a simple matter of logistics that no one single person would ever have enough time to visit them all in a lifetime. Indeed, an attempt to do such a thing would be meaningless.

Δ HIDDEN FORBIDDEN HOLY GROUND HULLE GRANZ CATHEDRAL

A cathedral stood on the lonely island in the middle of a dry, cauldronlike lake. The imposing stone building, lined with needlelike towers, was the kind of structure you could find in any fantasy RPG, a mixture of the styles of various eras, including Romanesque and Gothic. The bridge leading away from it did not reach to the far back of the dry lake, rather breaking off halfway over the lake bed, and this was where the teleportation terminal stood. Chaos Gates linked straight there.

Hulle Granz Cathedral. There was a special name for areas like this: Lost Grounds.

The areas to which Chaos Gates normally led comprised one of a selection of standard backgrounds, such as a grassy plain, a cave, or inside a building. These backdrops were used universally, with the map structure, monster level, content of treasure chests, and traps randomly generated for each. Mixed among these, however, were some areas that used a unique, single piece of scenery. There was no description or explanation of these special areas in the user manual or on the game's official site. These places, though part of The World, were not officially recognized as such. Thus, they had become known among the players as Lost Grounds. CC Corp itself did not acknowledge the existence of Lost Grounds. There were no monsters or treasures chests to be found there, and no events took place, making Lost Grounds totally pointless in terms of game progress—which served to stir up further questions about these locations among the players.

Long ago, this cathedral was where the humans enshrined the Goddess Aurora—not with prayers and offerings, but with terrible magic. Hulle Granz was where she was sealed away, and the eight chains wrapped around the statue of the goddess were said to be the embodiment of the eight curses that sealed her. Having obtained the power of the goddess for themselves, the humans turned to heaven, spat contemptuously, and used their new light to burn the gods who opposed them.

The history of humans . . . a history of sin.

We have sealed away the goddess, destroyed the gods, suppressed the other races, fought among ourselves, and found glory even as we've destroyed everything around us. And in the process, we all have forgotten the one truth: Those who sin eventually will be punished.

These shattered chains reflect our own future.

Before too long, humans would be wiped out . . . by human hands.

A shrine maiden once intoned this prophecy.

⬡ ⬡ ⬡

Amid the shafts of light slanting in through the windows of the central chamber stood a single Adept Rogue dressed all in black.

The sky was endlessly crimson.

Shino . . .

Ryou always thought of Shino here in the ruined cathedral.

"Long ago, there was a goddess statue here."

Shino had once told him this, right here.

"A goddess?"

"Aura, that's what she was called."

Why had Shino called the goddess Aura and not Aurora? Ryou, then still just starting out in the game, had no way of knowing. It wasn't a big mistake. Who cared about the background to an online game, anyway?

"What happened to it?"

The main pedestal in Hulle Granz Cathedral stood empty. The goddess statue that should have been there was gone; all that remained were eight shattered chains, scattered around the chamber.

The silver-haired, black-dressed Harvest Cleric had looked at the godless plinth before turning back to Haseo and offering a small smile.

"I guess she ran out of patience with this world."

That was Shino.

Compared to all the words Shino had left him with—words that he still remembered even after six months, that remained kind and beautiful within him, only growing in clarity with the passage of time—compared to that, just what was this Atoli girl, member of Moon Tree Guild, with her heartless, dull, meaningless diatribe? The words of that blonde, green-clothed copy of Shino were nothing more than hard, dry, stale old bread.

Yet they shared the same face.

Ryou was filled with a sudden, incomprehensible anger.

There was a hole in Ryou's heart, a Shino-shaped hollow, so beautiful and so twisted. Nothing else could possibly fill it.

Now a large triangle mark was scratched deeply into the holy plinth. It was almost as though a massive dragon had slashed the stone with its claws. This was the mark the PK Tri-Edge had left. . . .

Click, click.

"This game has a peculiar sort of autonomy."

Familiar footsteps rang out now, and the owner of the voice appeared in the shrine.

Ryou turned his game vision around to see the newcomer.

"It's been a while, Haseo . . . or should I say, Terror of Death?"

He was there. "Ovan . . ."

Ryou called Ovan's name while forcing down his overwhelming emotions. In the face of this light-hearted greeting, Ryou found he had a mountain of things to ask, and yet he couldn't find the words. Instead, he simply stood catching his breath.

Ovan walked down the central isle, passing by Haseo's side.

He was a Steam Gunner, a bayonet user. Whereas Haseo's height was about that of an average high school student, Ovan was a towering 6'2". He wore round dark glasses and clothing accented with white leather.

Then, there was his abnormal left arm.

Starting straight from his shoulder, Ovan's left arm was completely covered in a cylindrical part, like a metallic plaster cast. It looked like a mechanical prosthetic. It certainly wasn't part of the default PC design in The World.

Ovan was a mystery. Ryou know nothing of him in real life, either.

"You've become strong, much stronger than when I last saw you," Ovan said, stopping in front of the dais. "Back in the days of Twilight Brigade . . . You're like a totally different person now."

When Haseo had still been a fresh-faced beginner PC, he'd belonged to a guild called Twilight Brigade, led by Ovan as their

Guild Master. Shino had already been a member when he'd joined, and she'd taught him the ropes.

Turning to bring Ovan into view, Ryou—through Haseo—addressed the other PC's back.

"Becoming strong was my only choice. You and Shino were gone." *I was alone*, Ryou wanted to add, but he kept his self-pity to himself.

"Ovan, what have you been doing in the six months since disbanding the guild?"

The feeling that he'd been cast aside whirled in Ryou's heart. Ovan did not answer his question, however.

"It was just a small seed. There was only one way to find out what was inside . . . that's why I raised it."

"What does that mean?"

"Just a metaphorical side step." Ovan gave a nihilistic smile, talking in nothing but riddles. Ovan had always been like that. He never even tried to make his purpose or that of his guild clear. He created a feeling of his own presence, as well as expectation and centripetal force within the guild, simply by expecting things from his members, without telling them anything, without sharing anything with them. That was how Ovan did things.

"Where have you been? Why did you leave me alone?!" Ryou was sick of not being able to take action. He shouted, smashing his pent up feelings into Ovan's back.

He recalled what had happened half a year ago. Here. In this cathedral. *"I need to tell you about Shino . . ."*

● ⬡ ●

The meeting place with Shino had been this Lost Ground, Hulle Granz Cathedral.

When Haseo had hurried in, an ash gray Shino already was sprawled out there.

It was the scene of a brutal murder.

On the back of Shino's PKed corpse was a blazing, angry red, triangular wound.

And as though the attack had passed straight through her body, the same mark was burned into the dais.

The triangular mark had been there in Hulle Granz Cathedral ever since that day.

The PC Shino had been lost. And her player, Shino Nanao, had fallen into a mysterious coma. Ryou had learned this from the 'net news. One of her neighbors had heard a terrible scream and called the police. When they forced their way into Shino's apartment, they had found the girl unconscious, her M2D still on her head. She had no physical injuries, and there was no sign that anything had been stolen, so the incident was investigated as an accident rather than a crime.

At the time, it had been suggested that her coma could've resulted from excessive playing of an online game, or from shock due to extreme stress, but even now the definitive reason remained unknown.

Ryou believed that the basis for Shino Nanao's coma lay within The World.

He didn't have any concrete proof. And it was obvious from the start that such unscientific, groundless claims would be ignored even if he tried to share them with anyone, though this hadn't stopped him from contacting CC Corp countless times about Shino and the triangular scar that still remained. He hadn't received any sort of coherent reply.

Even as he struggled with his despair, Ryou was forced to carry on alone.

Because that triangle mark was *abnormal.*

It shouldn't be there. No mark caused by a PC attack should ever remain for so long in the scenery of The World. Ryou remained in The World in order to discover the reason behind that mark. That was why he couldn't stop being Haseo.

"This is where Shino . . ."

The one who left such triangular marks had become something of a myth among players of The World, so much so that he'd even been given a name.

"Tri-Edge. That's who this is about, isn't it?"

Ryou caught his breath when Ovan said the very name he'd just been thinking of.

Tri-Edge . . .

"What do you know about him?"

"A mysterious PK," Ovan started to speak quietly, standing in front of the Tri-Edge scar that was proof of Shino's death, "surrounded by azure flames . . ."

"Azure flames?"

Rumor had it that those killed by Tri-Edge were unable to ever return to the game.

"He's no ordinary PK. After being killed by Tri-Edge six months ago, Shino was not only unable to return to the game . . ." but her player had lost consciousness and was even now hospitalized, still in an unexplained coma.

"You know all of that . . . so why did you desert Shino, your guild, and me?"

Ryou's anger—and more than that, his anxiety—reached a breaking point. Why had the Guild Master he'd so looked up to, Ovan, someone who had been like his brother, known about Shino's sickness and still simply dropped out of contact? Why had he abandoned them?

"You're not confusing Shino with the lost goddess, are you? Is that why you've come here? To remember her? Your goddess?"

"That's enough!"

"So you became a PKK in order to track down Tri-Edge?" Rather than answer any of Ryou's questions, Ovan simply responded with queries of his own.

Ryou stared at Ovan with eyes overflowing with sadness and pain. He fixated on Ovan's player, someone whose real face and even name Ryou didn't know.

"I'm going to find Tri-Edge and uncover what he did to Shino."

That was the purpose that had supported Ryou for the past six months.

Ovan turned from the dais and fixed his gaze on Haseo.

"You have the guts to face Tri-Edge, do you?" His true intent, lurking behind those dark glasses, was difficult to ascertain.

"You bet I do!"

"He's about to return here, you see . . . to the scene of the tragedy."

"What? He's coming here?"

Ovan glanced up into nothingness for a moment, then stalked quickly past Haseo and headed for the Cathedral exit. "You are the only one I can trust with this."

Just as Ryou moved to head after him, a roar and a flash exploded out behind Haseo. He turned reflexively to investigate.

The Cathedral graphics were splintering away like a pane of shattered glass.

The display offered nothing for Haseo to see. And then, from amid the whirling void, there appeared . . . flames.

Blue flames.

There was life among the flame. Curled like a fetus, a figure now slowly opened one eye, surrounded as it was by flaming amniotic fluid.

A white eye surveyed its surroundings.

His arms out to the side, puncturing the flaming womb that surrounded him, he then floated down, landing gently on the ground.

His clothing was fluorescent orange, in tatters. More than just his clothing, his flesh and skin were also a zombielike patchwork, giving him a terrifying appearance. His basic model was barely recognizable as a young, slight PC, two swords in his hands.

Ryou's eyes opened wide in surprise when he saw the zombie held a weapon in each hand—and that the blades of the twisted, bizarrely shaped short swords suddenly divided into three with a dull metallic sound.

"Trident twin swords?" Triple-forked blades. Those violent triple prongs were burned blue into the back of Ryou's brain, the mark carved into the back of the dais and Ovan's words now all aligning. *"A mysterious PK surrounded by azure flames . . ."*

"Azure flames . . ."

Ryou swallowed. He tensed as though his heart had been plunged into ice water even as shock, anger, and joy bubbled up inside him.

"You're Tri-Edge?"

It seemed a pointless question.

The zombie, trident twin swords at the ready, closed in without speaking, exerting massive pressure on Haseo.

No reply . . . that settles it then. The zombie was going to fight. He was an enemy.

Haseo reflexively readied his twin swords and prepared to meet the attack.

"What did you do?" He targeted the zombie. "What did you do to Shino?"

His fingers moved over the controller.

Haseo attacked—and as soon as their blades clashed together, he knew the zombie was going to prove a tough adversary.

Now he was on the defensive. As he recovered from his own attack action, Haseo swapped equipment, switching to his chainsaw and ripping out a horizontal slash.

Sparks flew.

Nothing?

The zombie guarded again, and Haseo's attacks—actions that could kill a regular PC in a single blow—bounced off as though they were nothing. The zombie simply stood there, only moving one arm and yet still managing to stop every incoming strike, mocking and belittling with his limited motions.

No PC was programmed with such ability to insult with movement, so just *what was* this zombie?

It almost could have been all part of the game, a pre-scripted scene in an in-game event.

Ryou's goal was to find Tri-Edge and to extract from the PK exactly what he'd done to Shino, to find out why Shino was still in a coma. Ryou fought, asking questions as he did so. But the zombie replied to none of them.

What is this guy?

Just *what* was he? His emergence from the blue flames and everything else about him was irregular. Ryou was getting a very strange feeling about all this.

What he was doing, was it really just defending? Something seemed definitively wrong. It was like Haseo was in an RPG event battle, fighting an invincible monster, the only possible outcome defeat. It was abnormal in The World . . . strange and out of place.

The zombie launched a blazing attack, sending Haseo flying. He rolled helplessly across the ground, his face smashed into the floor.

He was knocked speechless.

Ryou had fought countless battles as Haseo, both as a regular player and then as the PKK known as the Terror of Death, but he had never experienced anything like this.

"What the hell?"

The scythe was gone from Haseo's right hand. The trident twin swords had destroyed Haseo's weapon.

This can't be happening!

Such a thing shouldn't have been possible. There was no such skill in The World's battle system, none that allowed you to destroy enemy equipment.

The zombie now loomed close, fully zoomed in on shaken Ryou's display, patchwork arms shuddering out at Tri-Edge's sides.

A brilliant flash spilled out complicated digital patterns, and then Ryou's brain was rocked inside his skull.

"Gaaaaaaaaaaaaaaaaaaaaaaaaaaaaaaaaaaaaaaaaaaaaaaaaaaaah!"

His consciousness faded amid a distant pain, as though he were in an endless freefall.

Excess waves rippled out from the shockwave of light, making the tatters of chains dance up into the air.

Small letters carved onto the chains danced across Ryou's M2D.

Skeith?

What was that? A name? Of what?

Then Ryou's world blacked out.

CHAPTER_02 : RAVEN

ONE

Eight months earlier, Ryou Misaki had logged into The World R:2 for the first time.

When Ryou's PC, Haseo, arrived in the Root Town, the message window in his sunglass-shaped M2D display immediately overflowed with other people's conversations, accompanied by a jumble of voices. The chat log scrolled smoothly past, sliding rapidly off the screen. Attempting to read all of this was the first source of panic for the fresh-faced beginner. It was like trying to listen to every conversation around you in the middle of a busy street.

Struggling with the unfamiliar controls, he swung the game camera this way and that. A highly detailed world spread out all around him.

Within the circular dome in which he'd appeared, there were men and women, large and small, humans as well as menlike beasts and creatures he couldn't even classify. These were the other PCs, controlled by players just as Haseo was controlled by Ryou. That was the "massively multiplayer" part of the game. Ryou slowly started to take it all in.

"Hey! You there."

Ryou didn't realize right away that this one voice was directed at him.

"Huh?"

"You there! Haseo! Is this your first time?" A friendly pair of PCs approached him, a cheerful-looking female swordsman and a banditlike youth whose hair was covered by his fringe.

"That's right, I guess." Ryou wondered for a moment how these two people he'd never seen before knew the name of his PC, but he soon figured it out. Targeting someone displayed the PC's name on the screen. The girl was called Asta and the youth was IYOTEN.

"Do not worry! Everyone has a first time. If you do not mind, we would like to help you out." Asta sounded a little stiff, a little formal.

"Actually, we'd love to help you out! Being kind to beginners isn't just a rule, it's good manners!" IYOTEN chipped in to the conversation.

Ryou didn't really know what to say, so he simply maintained his silence. The two of them just carried on regardless.

"That settles it then. We will start by giving you our member addresses."

A chime rang out, along with the appearance of a system message indicating that Haseo had obtained the member addresses of both IYOTEN and Asta.

"Let me explain about member addresses. . . ."

Member addresses were the business cards of The World. Ryou, still a total beginner, went along with what the other two told him and gave them his member address, too, thus forming a party. Asta's and IYOTEN's names then appeared on his status screen. Given their levels, it seemed they were both quite experienced players.

"Look at that." Asta pointed. Pointing was a simple movement for a PC if the proper motion commands were registered in advance—but as a beginner, Ryou had more pressing issues on his mind.

A rotating ball of light hovered in the center of the circular dome.

"That is called a Chaos Gate. It is a teleportation device that allows access to areas other than this Root Town," Asta continued her explanation.

Ryou had no idea what he was doing, really, so he just selected the three keyword phrases as he was told.

"'Courageous,' 'Engaging,' and 'Daydream.' Those three will do." IYOTEN smiled. He reassured Haseo that it was an area specifically designed for beginner players, so even at level 1, he would be fine.

"You do not speak much, do you?" Asta shrugged. Experienced players made skillful use of character motions during conversation. That was all part of the "role play."

"Voice chat is there for a reason, you know."

"Let's have some fun, okay?"

With both of them urging him on, and not wanting to put a damper on the mood, Ryou spoke loudly into the microphone on his M2D.

"Okay!"

He selected the commands they indicated to him, and Haseo was surrounded by a ring of light and teleported away with his two new party members.

△ COURAGEOUS ENGAGING DAYDREAM

The instant after his display blacked out, Ryou found Haseo standing on a verdant green plain. He had been teleported from the Root Town to the area △ Courageous Engaging Daydream.

"Let's go grab some treasure!"

"Look, monsters!"

A handful of monsters were positioned to block a nearby bridge. They were ugly little humanoid creatures. Ryou targeted them to see their monster name, Goblin Rookie, displayed.

"Perfect for a little training for you, Haseo."

Ryou proceeded to work his way through the area, following the advice of his two new friends. His first battle with monsters. He checked the direction the monsters were facing and attacked from behind to get a "surprise attack" bonus. He learned how to attack and how to use skills, as well as how to heal. If he slipped up,

Asta and IYOTEN were there to back him up. In that way, Haseo gradually worked his way through the monsters. Ryou proved to be a quick learner.

"Good work!"

"You are doing very well!"

Before he even realized it, Haseo and his party had wiped all the monsters off the map.

"I do have one question," Haseo interjected.

"Yeah?"

"I thought an Adept Rogue could use multiple weapons?"

He'd read that in the description on the character creation screen, but Haseo was only equipped with twin swords.

"Ah, you are an Adept Rogue." Asta went on to explain the system. Although as an Adept Rogue, Haseo would eventually be capable of equipping multiple weapons, at the beginning, he could use only one type of weapon. He would have to clear a special event called a Job Extend in order to be able to use and equip the other two types.

"You don't have to worry about that gig just yet, Haseo," IYOTEN said. Haseo would need to level up first.

"Why did you select the Adept Rogue, anyway?"

"I thought it'd be fun to use a lot of different equipment."

Asta and IYOTEN both started to laugh when they heard this reply.

Ryou only learned later that Adept Rogues were one of the least popular character types in The World, if not *the* least popular.

They took a long time to level up, and still ended up with middling weapon stats—at least, that's what most people thought. His childlike response in conjunction with that knowledge had been more than enough to elicit laughter from the two more experienced players.

At the time, not knowing exactly what was so funny, Ryou simply worried that he'd maybe done something wrong.

"Shall we finish with a trip to the Shrine then?" asked Asta.

"Shrine?"

"The Beast God's Shrine. There's treasure to be had there." IYOTEN cheekily stuck out his tongue.

● ◆ ●

The Beast God's Shrine looked like a ruin from South America. They headed down the stairs from its entrance, arriving at an underground dais surrounded by blazing torches.

Three sets of footsteps proceeded into the shrine.

"That is Alvinel, the God of Judgment," Asta pointed out. A massive statue, like a giant monster, floated in the air in the Shrine, obviously a result of some sort of magic. "A newer god in The World, he is said to lead those duly qualified into the kingdom of the gods . . . or something like that. Everyone has their own theories, anyway."

After this explanation of the game's official settings, IYOTEN added his own slant. "We simply call him 'the Item God,' though." He gave a dry laugh.

Ryou vaguely recalled something about gods and wars between races in the game manual he'd downloaded. But he shared his new companions' disinterest in such game background.

"Do you see the treasure chest in front of the statue? There should be a nice item in there."

"Open it and see. Go on."

"You're sure?" Haseo asked, even as they spurred him on.

"If you're willing to risk the wrath of the god, yeah."

The kind of items that were to be found in areas aimed at beginners probably wouldn't interest the two of them. Ryou decided to accept their kindness. He ran Haseo over to the front of the statue of Alvinel.

Haseo looked up, targeting the chest in front of the massive statue. It opened.

Having now obtained his first item from his first quest, Ryou found himself unable to stop smiling.

"Thank you!" He turned back toward the other players, filled with nothing but honest, naïve thanks . . . but found his display was filled by the tip of a sword.

"You're here for the treasure," IYOTEN smiled, waving his sword, "and we are here for *you*."

Asta pointed at Haseo as though he were a joke.

"What . . . what do you mean?" Ryou was taken aback.

"To wipe out a fleeing, bleating little lamb in the blink of an eye. How good that feels." IYOTEN sounded like a bad actor in a second-rate crime drama.

"Idiots like you shouldn't be allowed into this game in the first place." Now he sounded like a street punk.

"Hey! You promised I would get to do the killing this time!" Asta's voice was loaded with malice. "He is my prize."

Ryou was stuck dumb by the sudden, unexpected change in these two, who until now had just been kind, friendly, more experienced players. The hands that gripped his controller slicked up with cold sweat. He had no idea what was going on. He just wanted to run . . . desperately wanted to get away. Giving in to his base instincts, he started Haseo running.

IYOTEN moved easily to block him.

Outside. He had to get outside the Beast God Shrine!

"Hel——!" Ryou started to shout, but then Asta appeared in his way.

She lifted a massive broad sword—bigger than herself and fitted with countless revolving saws—and didn't hesitate to slice Haseo in two with a single cut.

An ash gray Haseo filled Ryou's display.

PK.

Ryou would later learn that there were players who chose to kill other players. He only realized that he'd been tricked just before his PC had died. His controller no longer responded, giving him no choice but to watch as his alter ego was brutally cut down.

IYOTEN and Asta moved over to Haseo's body.

"Not much of a challenge, was he?"

"I guess we can't expect anything more from a beginner."

Their murderous intent now on full display, it was obvious that their desire for evil was not yet fulfilled, Haseo having died from a single blow. So they proceeded to kick his body.

"It's like snapping a chick's neck . . . that's why I can't quite find enjoyment in the newbies!"

Even as IYOTEN continued beating the corpse, it was suddenly swept away, voice and all, by a brilliant ribbon of light.

Asta flinched at the sound of a gun.

What's happening . . . ? Ryou had no idea.

IYOTEN was blasted clear out of Haseo's line of sight. Asta was already scanning the entrance of the shrine for the PC who'd fired the shot.

"Who the hell're you?" Asta was obviously shaken, for she even dropped her more formal speech. In the next instant, her body was doubled over, bent by another blast of devouring light.

Silence settled across the Beast God Shrine. Both IYOTEN and Asta had been taken out with a single shot each.

Footsteps rang out.

From his fixed viewpoint staring up at the ceiling, Ryou finally looked upon the one who'd killed Haseo's PKs: Amid the light filtering down from the ceiling, a Steam Gunner offered his hand to Haseo.

"Welcome to The World."

That was how Haseo and Ovan had met.

Having been resurrected by Ovan, Haseo accepted his invitation to join his guild, Twilight Brigade. There, he would meet Shino, who was already a member.

TWO

The chirps of cicadas filled the air. Outside the window was a dazzling blue sky, and the sound of a train passing in the distance could be faintly heard.

The residential district along the Keio line stretched out into the suburbs. . . .

Ryou lifted his head up from his desk, leaving a trail of dribble. His head spun dizzily. He shivered. His temples throbbed. Maybe he had set the air conditioning too high, because every joint of his body ached as though he were suffering from a nasty cold.

Ryou wiped his mouth with the back of his hand. Then he snapped back to himself, snatching the sunglasslike M2D display from his head and looking around.

He was in his room.

It was summer holiday.

Ryou had pulled an all-nighter playing The World. Getting addicted to an online game totally paralyzed your sense of time in the real world. It was already morning. His slow, sluggish brain struggled back to life, thinking over everything that had happened the night before.

After taking out the PK party led by that redhead, he'd encountered Sakaki and Atoli from Moon Tree Guild in Mac Anu and entered into a fairly one-sided debate. Then he'd received mail from Ovan, pointing him toward the Lost Ground of Hulle Granz Cathedral. There, he'd met Ovan again and . . .

"Tri-Edge!"

He'd been attacked by that patchwork zombie PC wielding trident twin swords. Haseo had been defeated in a totally one-sided battle. The last thing he remembered was the zombie's hand . . . the hand of the PK Tri-Edge spreading across his display. And then, Ryou's consciousness had been blown out in a flash of light.

"I lost consciousness . . . ?"

He pressed between his eyebrows, hard enough that his nails hurt.

It hadn't been light yet when he'd been playing. And yet now it was morning. That left a blank couple of hours in Ryou's memory. He'd lost consciousness, definitely. And this was more than simply dropping offline due to falling asleep.

Exactly the same as Shino!

Now he was totally back to himself.

He must've been on the verge of falling into the same kind of coma as Shino Nanao. That zombie with the trident twin swords and his veil of azure flames was Tri-Edge, the very PK who'd rendered Shino unconscious. Ryou was now finally convinced that the reason for Shino Nanao's coma lay within The World.

But he still didn't know what it was.

Yet Ryou himself had blacked out, and Shino had spent the last six month in bed.

He grabbed the M2D display from where it had tumbled onto his desk.

He couldn't let Tri-Edge escape. After six months of wandering through The World, he'd finally found the one responsible for Shino's condition. He wasn't going to give up now.

Taking up the controller again, Ryou made his way back into The World.

△ SERVER ROOT TOWN: THE ETERNAL CITY OF MAC ANU

Having logged in again, Ryou immediately tried to return to Hulle Granz Cathedral, the site of his encounter with Tri-Edge.

He hurried to the Chaos Gate and input the words . . . and then, he noticed something odd.

Hold on . . . ?

Something was wrong with Haseo's appearance.

A slight, youthful PC stood there. The black armored Adept Rogue—the PKK renowned as the Terror of Death, the level 133 idol to which Ryou had sacrificed his life—was gone . . . leaving nothing but a newbie PC, the same as the first time he'd ever logged in, a character that hadn't even performed his Job Extend yet.

Level 1?

He checked his status and was immediately rendered speechless. His weapon was back to its initial settings. No items. All the member addresses he'd gathered were gone, too.

Eight long months.

The massive amount of time Ryou had poured into Haseo and The World was totally gone.

Ryou quickly descended into panic. His attachment to The World all had been to save the comatose Shino—and knowing no other way, having no other leads, he'd simply spent his days continuing to level up as he searched for Tri-Edge. Days spent thirsting for more power. And now it was all gone.

"I can't believe it!"

Ryou logged out again.

From the title screen, he opened the mail program directly connected to The World. Another terrible blow. All his mail was gone. All his messages from Shino, too—even the one setting up their first in-person meeting.

All the evidence that Haseo had shared his existence with Shino . . . gone.

Ryou trembled. His hands shook. His consciousness started to leak away like water from a cracked vase, replaced with a viscous darkness that crept into his heart.

He had no idea what was happening, had no idea what to do next.

"I know . . . Ovan." He was the only one Ryou could turn to. Ovan would know what to do. Ryou quickly logged in again.

He tried sending a personal message to Ovan, but Ovan had already logged out, so the message couldn't be sent. He tried visiting Hulle Granz Cathedral again, but there was no sign of Tri-Edge.

Ryou felt as though his chest were going to tear in two.

Tri-Edge had stolen Shino from him, and now Haseo, who'd been like Ryou's other half. Taken so simply, too, as though mocking his struggles over the last six months.

As he walked dazed through Mac Anu, two PCs suddenly talked to Haseo.

"Are you a new player?"

"Would you like to form a party with us?"

This was the start to a typical, everyday exchange in The World. But hearing these words, Ryou was suddenly, painfully reminded of the pair of newbie hunters he'd encountered after logging in for the first time.

"Uwaaaah!" He screamed and made Haseo run.

Run. Run. Run. He blasted through the streets as though something had gone wrong in his head. He dashed left and then right through the labyrinthine city of Mac Anu. The evening city on his display looked like nothing less than a nightmare to Ryou.

His confusion eventually turned into a strange fear, a fear he could not explain.

"Hey?"

A nightmare reunion, too.

Having arrived at in a dead-end alley, Haseo was confronted by a number of PCs.

Ryou flinched back. This particular dead-end alley was occupied by a woman with frizzy red hair—Bordeaux—and her group of PKs that Haseo had taken out the night before.

"Haseo?"

"The Terror of Death?"

The PKs flinched back, too.

But after a moment . . . taking in Haseo's new appearance . . .

"Hold on . . ."

The PKs beyond the display stabbed into Ryou's heart with their unseen eyes.

Don't look. Don't look at me! Ryou almost felt like shouting wildly.

"Bordeaux, check it out!"

"Level 1?"

The PKs looked unbelievingly at Haseo. Of course they did. Haseo, who just yesterday had appeared as the prince of devils, the demon among demons, was now a fresh-faced beginner PC again.

They didn't know why, of course. Ryou himself had no idea why.

But the PKs were quick to grab at the heart of the matter: the simple fact that they were now faced with someone weaker than them.

"Oh, it's been too long, Haseo! I'm amazed at the *change* in you." Bordeaux stared intently at Haseo.

"Hey, I think I've got it!" Negimaru clapped his hands as though suddenly working something out. "His illegal activities have been found out by CC Corp and he's been kicked back to level 1!"

"Hey! You think?" There was a streak of happiness in Bordeaux's voice.

"We were just talking about you, actually! You kicked mud in our faces, boy, mud in the faces of Kestrel Guild, and we were trying to work out how to pay you back." Negimaru was getting pretty serious.

Kestrel was the largest guild in The World. It had more than five thousand members. It was known for its aggressive attitude, and many of its members were PKs. Some even compared them to the mafia. Staying on their good side was vital in order to enjoy the game.

"I've been playing all night, and I'm ready to pop! Right, Bordeaux?"

"We can't PK here, though . . . isn't that a shame?" Bordeaux sidled up to Ryou, as though reading the deepest fears in his heart.

"But I've got a treat for the boards here. The pathetic little Terror of Death, now a level 1 newbie! The price for his cheating, paid in full!"

A passing insult from Negimaru had now become fact. All cheaters were treated like top-level criminals by other players in MMORPGs like The World.

"Stroll through the town to booing and catcalls! Head into any area and the PKs will descend! You'll never want to log in again once we're finished with you! You've lost your place in The World, buddy!"

It was baseless fiction, but the truth didn't matter. These were the ones who would swarm like white ants over the weak, the helpless, devouring them.

"I'm gonna love you so hard that you'll never forget it, that you'll see me in your dreams, that your mind is gonna break, baby. . . ." That was Bordeaux's revenge.

Ryou couldn't reply. He felt lost, small, weak. Just yesterday, all five thousand Kestrel members at once wouldn't have scared him.

But his confidence was now gone, vanished along with his experience points. The Terror of Death, Haseo, was now nothing more than a coward, scared of even his own shadow.

What else can I do . . . ?

Unable to bear it, Ryou scrambled to select the logout command.

Why? Why am I running?

It would be throwing away Haseo. It would be the same as throwing away his fight to save Shino. He couldn't do that. Haseo was exposed here. It was a strange twist of fate.

"You don't belong here. Get out of this area!" Negimaru threatened, but a voice broke in.

"Stop there."

Haseo spun around. Standing in the entrance to the alley was a female PC. She was a Tribal Grappler. Her hair was bright pink and tied up in two large pigtails. She was wearing glasses and a necktie, too. It was very "fetish style." Her curvaceous figure was barely covered by her costume.

"Who the hell do you think you are?" Negimaru spat out.

"It is against the user agreement to persistently target or abuse a particular player, even if verbally," the pink-haired Tribal Grappler stated firmly, her arms crossed. She looked resolute, and the PKs were left to come to their own conclusions.

"You're a . . . GM?"

GMs, or Game Masters, were PCs operated by employees of CC Corp. Some were full-time employees, and others were only part-timers. They performed a lot of roles in The World, from overseeing the smooth running of major in-game events to mediating in disputes between players.

"I'm just a player, but I did hear you verbally abusing him."

She could have read it all in the log, which converted voice to text as it scrolled up in her text message window. It was like a Dictaphone, recording everything they said.

"Wha—?"

"Even if I'm not a GM, I could notify a guild that despises PKs like yourselves."

The PKs buzzed at this.

"Moon Tree Guild? Are you going to report us?" Bordeaux thundered.

The pink-haired Tribal Grappler made a shrugging motion. "Maybe I will. Maybe I won't."

"Bordeaux, what are we going to do?" Negimaru sounded worried. He could tell they weren't going to win this argument. It didn't look like Bordeaux was going to be able to rely on her lackeys when faced with this enemy.

"We don't want to get in trouble with Moon Tree Guild," Bordeaux tutted. Her minions were pathetic, but even she was starting to back off a little now. She knew well that Moon Tree Guild and Kestrel Guild were the powers in The World, although they were located at the opposite extremes of opinion. Bordeaux herself wanted to avoid unnecessary conflict between them wherever possible, although she wouldn't admit that to anyone else very often.

"I'll remember this!" Negimaru howled.

"Oh, really?"

"Yeah!"

And with that final exchange, Bordeaux left. Her henchmen soon followed, muttering similar curses.

Haseo was finally safe, but Ryou didn't really know what to say now.

"Idiots . . . I saved you all," she muttered.

Ryou didn't really understand what the pink Tribal Grappler was muttering about.

She turned around to face him. "Well then, Ryou."

Dadum. At the voice, Ryou's heart skipped.

What? He'd never felt that before. He felt a piercing pain as if there were a swelling tumor somewhere deep in his chest. It was most definitely caused by the Tribal Grappler standing in front of him, though.

"How do you know my name?"

Trying to fight back the strange feeling inside, Ryou clicked on the details for the female Tribal Grappler who'd come to his rescue. Her name was Pi.

"You're right, I owe you an explanation. Actually, I've been watching you for a long time." Pi wasn't really making things clearer for Ryou. It made him even more suspicious of her, but he tried to maintain his composure so that it didn't show.

"Usually, people at least tell me their names first," Haseo said.

"Heh. You're just as stubborn as they say." Pi smiled.

"You know about me? Are you like a fan or something?"

"I'm not into kids."

"And I'm not into old women," Ryou countered Pi's insult.

"O-old?!" Pi managed to stop herself from going any further, issuing a sigh instead.

"All I've heard from you so far is complaining. Real old woman."

"How dare you! I'm—" Pi's voice was rising, but when she realized she was falling into Ryou's trap, she quickly pulled back.

"What did you want then?" Ryou smirked.

"I want to invite you to our headquarters." Pi got straight to the point.

"What? Headquarters?"

"I'm a member of Raven Guild. We may be able to help you in your search for Tri-Edge."

Dadum. Ryou's heart skipped a beat again.

"What the hell do you know?" He couldn't hide his excitement. Now that she'd mentioned the name Tri-Edge, there was no way that Ryou could refuse her invitation.

●　⬡　●

THREE

@HOME were headquarters for guilds within The World. A shared door appeared in one part of each Root Town. When you selected the name of the guild you were in, the door would transfer you to your guild's @HOME screen, each of which was designed to look like rooms under a city, very much resembling a secret hideout. Members of the guild could store items in the @HOME warehouse, buy goods from the guild shop, and also use commands for activities such as weapon training. Using the guild ranking system within The World, guild members could earn points, thus increasing the guild's rank and unlocking more functions at the @HOME location.

Pi had given Ryou Raven Guild's @KEY so that he could access the guild's headquarters, and once he'd input the @KEY, he'd been transferred to Raven Guild's @HOME screen.

It was a guild @HOME of ordinary rank. Raven appeared to be a fairly small guild, similar to Twilight Brigade, which Ryou had been a member of.

"So, what is it?"

No one besides Pi and Ryou occupied the @HOME.

Pi ignored Haseo and walked to the back of the room. The layout of Raven's @HOME followed the standard template; therefore, the door she was opening should have led to a small room where members could do weapon training. However, when Haseo passed through the door, he was met with a black screen.

When the blackness faded away, Haseo was standing on a stone floor. The entire place was so dark that he couldn't see three steps in front of him. In the space he could see at all, he could only make out the floor. He couldn't tell how large the room was even . . . it just faded into the dark. It could have gone on forever. Conspicuously absent was the typical @HOME BGM.

"Huh?"

Pi made no reply. She had come through the same door, so she should've been transferred to the same area. This was a MMORPG. This was The World. Nothing unusual should have been occurring there.

Then the space broke. Around Haseo, several windows opened. Inside the windows, video playbacks were displayed.

"Wha—?!"

They showed Haseo himself . . . with Bordeaux from Kestrel, Atoli and Sakaki from Moon Tree, and even Ovan.

"You've been monitoring me?" Ryou was shocked.

All the scenes had been shot from overhead cameras, unseen by their ignorant targets, as they'd been positioned higher than any PC could jump.

"Ryou Misaki, seventeen. Lives in Tokyo. Second year student at a prestigious high school. Father is the manager of a leading company. Eight months playing The World R:2. PC character name is Haseo. Once a member of Twilight Brigade, but now a lone PKK. Otherwise known as the Terror of Death."

Pi emerged from the darkness. She was the one who'd been reciting Ryou's personal information.

Ryou couldn't speak. He was taken aback that she seemed to know all his personal details. He felt violated.

"Last night, you lost consciousness while playing The World."

In the final window, there was the image of a zombie in the Hulle Granz Cathedral—and also the image of Haseo, defeated by Tri-Edge. Tri-Edge had the palm of his hand open. His hand was omitting a pulse of light.

"That is a skill called Data Drain."

"Data . . . Drain?"

Ryou had never heard of it. If there were such a skill, and it could render another play to lose consciousness, then . . .

"It defies reason." Suddenly, a voice came from above their heads.

All the video windows closed. At the same time, a glowing light issued from the wall of darkness. An uroboros—a snake biting its tail—shone on the back of the wall like some ancient carving. It was magnificent and elegant. Like a mandala, it worked from small details in the center to a massive world view along the outer edges.

Ryou was rendered speechless.

Was this really The World? How could this data exist at the back of Raven's @HOME? Ryou had never seen anything like it. Ryou was frustrated by his lack of knowledge of The World, but also by a strange sense of foreboding that he couldn't quite place. It was as if there were something unknown hiding in this game. Then, a lotus-shaped platform like the pedestal of a Buddhist statue descended from above. Standing on it was a single PC.

"Yata."

Pi greeted him with a nod. The PC was muscular and tanned. His head was shaved, and he wore a cloth around his body like a monk. In his hand, he held a fan, marking him as a Macabre Dancer.

"Welcome to the Serpent of Lore."

The male Macabre Dancer, Yata, stopped and gazed down at the younger PC, Haseo, with a look of curiosity.

Serpent of Lore must be the name of this area, Ryou thought to himself. And from Pi's evident deference to this man, he determined Yata must be the Guild Master of Raven.

"Who the hell are you people?" Haseo challenged Pi and Yata.

"Yes, it is all a bit too much to take in." Yata sympathized with him, and this calmed Ryou into silence. The monklike Macabre Dancer started to calmly explain: "Within The World, anomalies exist. They can manifest as events or within subjects; there are various forms. They're not supposed to be in The World. These illegal phenomena have come to be known collectively as AIDA."

"AIDA?"

The word that Ryou said didn't appear in the text box. It wasn't recorded in the general dictionary that The World used for voice recognition.

"AIDA are still not commonly known among ordinary players. But Haseo, *you* know them . . . and the threat that AIDA pose." As Yata trailed off, a new video window opened.

The screen displayed a hospital bed. Laying on it was a thin girl—Shino Nanao, shown from several different angles.

Ryou was shocked again.

The video of the unconscious player was interrupted by the appearance of another PC in the Serpent of Lore. This time, it was a Harvest Cleric PC.

"Shino . . ."

It was the corpse of PC Shino—but it wasn't a real corpse. The PC's black costume was slashed, her golden hair, her skin, her entire body covered in black spots, like a plague victim.

"Shino Nanao is another player who fell into a coma after an incident involving an AIDA phenomena. We call these victims Lost Ones."

"You recovered Shino's PC?"

Ryou exploded with emotion. They'd been secretly recording Shino in her sickbed and keeping her corpse as if it were a plaything! Even if it were only a PC, he felt it mocked the real Shino's situation. In front of the pathetic, lifeless figure of a loved one, Ryou was filled with rage at Pi, Yata, and Raven. He could kill them right there and then! Internally, he screamed.

I AM.

That wasn't Ryou's voice.

The M2D speakers made a strange noise, almost as if the voice were coming from inside Ryou's head. He thought that he recognized it. Confused, Ryou grabbed the M2D with both hands.

Who are you?

He felt something . . . someone was standing with him. The owner of the voice was behind him! Ryou instinctively swung around in real life.

In a state of shock, Ryou couldn't tell if what he was sensing was behind Haseo's back or behind Ryou Misaki's back, because it was behind him both offline and online.

I AM HERE.

No, the voice was coming from inside him. Was it Ryou Misaki's? No . . . Was it Haseo's?

"We want to find the cause of it."

Ryou could still hear Yata talking serenely, despite being lost in the sensation of being somewhere between his online and offline personas. Slowly, he regained control of himself.

"Haseo, we want your cooperation with Raven Guild regarding the issue of the Lost Ones."

"Cooperation?" Ryou glared at Pi. "You have to be kidding me! I'm not associating with people who put spy cameras in hospitals! Who the hell do you think you are? And what the hell is up with your @HOME?! You used a cheat? You must have!" A stream of abuse issued from Haseo, flooding the chat box.

"Do as you will."

"Ngh." Ryou was irritated that his abuse didn't seem to have any effect on Yata.

"Are you sure, Yata?" Pi purposefully made a motion to push her glasses up her nose, indicating that she was incredulous.

"He has nowhere to go. Haseo, you must realize that, too."

Yata and Pi then turned to each other and started to talk about "Epitaphs" and "awakenings."

Ryou didn't really understand.

"Epitaphs?" What were those? Ryou felt like everything had been turned upside down. AIDA, Lost Ones . . . it hurt him that he didn't understand these words. He felt so powerless in front of the comatose Shino, whom, no matter how hard he tried, he couldn't find a way to save.

"One word of advice," Pi said. "Haseo, your PC hides a dangerous power."

"What?"

"Have you heard a voice coming from inside your PC? We have the ability to control that power."

Voice.

In his rage, Ryou slammed down on the key to log out and threw the M2D against the wall.

CHAPTER_03 : POSSESSION

ONE

No desire to go into the light, only deference to the light.

Eternal sunset or dawn? Either way, the sun cleansed Hulle Granz Cathedral.

At the back of the inner sanctum, there was a single window.

"Lost Grounds?" Ryou asked. Shino was next to him, Shino when he had first met her. Haseo hadn't been in The World for long when Shino had invited him to the Lost Ground for sightseeing.

"Every now and then, they discover them."

"Discover?"

"Discover" was the best way to describe finding these special areas and maps such as Hulle Granz Cathedral. These places were called Lost Grounds.

"This was probably an event area," Ryou guessed.

"But they couldn't clear this."

According to Shino, there were several Lost Grounds. They were unique areas, but they weren't used for world events. In fact, nothing official happened on Lost Grounds. Consequently, players couldn't help but feel discomfort. They couldn't understand why the programmers had prepared areas without a single usable resource and where no events were held.

"It's a strange place."

"Yeah." Shino nodded.

Without purpose, it seemed to break the promise of the RPG. The game administrators at CC Corp appeared to tolerate the existence of Lost Grounds, though.

"Are they just a feature to get people talking?" Ryou asked Shino.

"Could be."

"It's not just that?"

"It's romantic." Shino giggled. She was always laughing. She passed the altar, where a plinth stood without a statue.

Ryou was entranced as he watched Shino, bathed in light and visible through his display

"A long time ago, there used to be a statue of a goddess here," Shino said.

"A goddess?" Ryou asked.

"She was called Aura."

"Aura?"

For some reason that word appeared in Roman characters in his text chat, not the usual kanji.

"The name of the goddess of light. The mythical one."

Ryou thought that Shino must be talking about the background story of The World.

"Goddess . . ."

There was no statue there now, though. And however beautiful the place was, it was nothing but ruins. The strange emptiness of the plinth made the whole place feel even more deserted and empty. It was strange—but perhaps the creators had intended it to be this way.

"What happened to it?" Ryou asked.

"I guesss she ran out of patience with this world."

Shino turned around, and as she did, another voice came from the entrance of the cathedral.

"This game has a peculiar sort of autonomy."

It was Ovan. The day that Ryou first logged into The World, he'd dealt with two PKs who'd preyed on beginners. They had PKed Haseo, but Ovan had resurrected the PC and invited him into the guild he ran.

"Autonomy?"

"Parts of the game aren't run by any of CC Corp's protocols, rather by the rules of the game itself."

Ovan's footsteps echoed as he walked down the nave, approaching Shino and Haseo.

"I don't understand."

"The item that Twilight Brigade seeks is the Key of the Twilight. It wasn't something CC Corp created in the game, rather something The World itself created."

"Is that possible?"

Ryou couldn't believe it. What *was* this game? The World seemed to have taken on a life of its own. Ovan and Shino were taking this MMORPG as seriously as real life.

"It exists." Ovan was dead serious.

"Huh?"

"Or at least that's the assumption under which our Twilight Brigade plays the game."

Shino smiled at Ovan's words. "I'm sure the goddess exists, too."

Ryou felt like he was being mocked, and it upset him.

● ⬡ ●

Here he was again . . . Haseo had arrived at Hulle Granz Cathedral.

For Ryou, this was a place for confrontation, and not with a goddess. When this empty cathedral shone in his eyes, it reflected what he had lost—Shino, Twilight Brigade, and Ovan.

And here, finally, Haseo had found Shino's foe, Tri-Edge.

But Haseo had been defeated, and both Ryou and Haseo had lost everything as a result. Ryou rejected it and was dejected by it. He'd lost sight of the path in his solitude.

"Data Drain?"

He remembered what Pi and Yata of Raven had told him the night before, about the illegal skill that had come from Tri-Edge's hand and had reduced Ryou to a level I PC again.

For the half a year that Shino had been unconscious, or a Lost One, Ryou had neglected his real life and put all his effort into this online game. He'd been obsessed with leveling up and obtaining the power in Haseo to prove his feelings for Shino. Tri-Edge had taken all that away in an instant. This weakling level I PC felt like a corpse to him.

"I lost to Tri-Edge."

The past half a year was for nothing.

Alone, he unsheathed his blades. The points of his swords were aimed at the ceiling of the cathedral as Haseo searched for an absent enemy.

Like an illusion, Tri-Edge.

Ryou's heart was empty.

"I need power. Shino . . ." He searched for something, gripping the controller in his hand. "An undefeatable power."

He needed something that couldn't be lost or borrowed, something more than data and figures, which could be reduced to zero. But there was no way that was going to be possible, and his own foolishness stung deep.

● ◆ ●

TWO

ΔROOT TOWN: THE ETERNAL CITY OF MAC ANU

When Ryou first started playing The World, Twilight Brigade had helped him level up. He'd progressed through the levels with the help of Shino, a Harvest Cleric. But when Ovan disappeared, Haseo left the guild and went solo to become a PKK. His real aim was to find a way to help the unconscious Shino, and he didn't need friends to help him. Playing alone, Haseo had reached the insanely high level of 133.

However, now he was back at the level of a beginner. It was as if he'd very suddenly aged. He had no guild to help him now, either. The lowest goblins could kick him around like a piece of trash, and he had no means to stand up to the despicable PKs.

Haseo returned to the Root Town and was wandering about aimlessly when something in the corner of the display caught Ryou's eye.

He sensed that someone was watching him. He was really sensitive to other people watching him now, like a pathetic sniveling little animal. It was humbling.

Sure enough, a single PC approached him, parting the crowd that was gathered in front of the circular hall in front of the Chaos Gate.

"Um . . ." It was the voice of a small child.

The PC was wearing a crescent-shaped hat and some very eccentric clothing. Ryou judged by the voice that the player must've been around ten. However, because of the voice software, it was impossible to tell if the PC was really controlled by a child player.

He was a Shadow Warlock, and his PC name was Sakubo.

"Um, you're a beginner, right?"

Ryou didn't answer the question. Haseo may have been a level 1, but Ryou wasn't. Sakubo must have mistaken his silence to mean Haseo was simply nervous because he was a beginner.

"Let me help you!"

"What?" Haseo couldn't stop himself.

"I'm in a guild that helps new players. It's called Canard. We have to help as many people as possible!"

This kid apparently was in a guild that focused on helping new players.

"I can help you."

Ryou ignored him and was about to leave the hall. However, the child Shadow Warlock let out a little yelp and ran after him.

"Wait . . . please wait!"

Sakubo chased him outside. Haseo tried to slip through the crowd to lose him. There were a lot of pushy playing styles around these days. That fake Shino was pushy, too. . . .

Ngh! Without thinking, Ryou pulled his hand away from the controller. On the railing of the large bridge over Mac Anu's waterway, there she stood, the fake Shino—Atoli of Moon Tree.

"HELP THE CAMPAIGN FOR THE ABOLITION OF PKING!" she yelled. She'd put her character into shout mode. Atoli's speech came up in large letters, so that all the PCs on the street would be able to see it.

"HELP THE CAMPAIGN FOR THE ABOLITION OF PKING. PLEASE SIGN THE PETITION!"

Moon Tree's political motives were to get CC Corp to prohibit PK actions. Part of this campaign was to collect signatures on a digital petition they had on their site.

"IF YOU'RE INTERESTED, THEN PLEASE VISIT MOON TREE'S OFFICIAL WEBSITE AT—"

"SHUT UP!" A scream interrupted Atoli, leaving her shaken. Surrounding Atoli were a couple of thuggish-looking men.

"Will you shut up with your racket?"

"AIEE!" Atoli let out a yelp.

And then, Haseo suddenly noticed something. *Those two . . .*

The red-haired girl . . . they were the PK Bordeaux's lackeys. One of them was a Twin Blade with his hair done up at the top, the other a beefy-looking Edge Punisher . . . Negimaru and Grein. It looked as if Atoli also remembered that these were the two who'd tried to PK her before.

"Where did you say you're from . . . ?"

"Moon Tree Guild," Negimaru spat out in disgust.

Bordeaux and her friends were all part of the militant guild Kestrel. Atoli was a member of the pacifist guild Moon Tree. The two mixed like water and oil.

"HELP THE CAMPAIGN FOR THE ABOLITION OF PKING!" Atoli turned to the PKs and started shouting again.

Atoli certainly had guts, Ryou had to give her that.

Negimaru clearly hadn't expected that response, though, as he was lost for words for a moment. However, after a few seconds of silence, he burst out laughing. "Mwahahaha."

"What?" Atoli demanded an explanation.

"Are you stupid or something? I think you need to see a doctor offline, missy." He gestured, spinning circles with his finger near his temple. And then Negimaru laughed again.

It was indeed a bit crazy to deliberately work up what were effectively killers in this world. But Atoli fell quiet at being called insane, and Negimaru and Grein left, looking very self-satisfied.

Atoli's small, courageous show of defiance and Negimaru's mocking disappeared up the log as the voices of the crowd continued. And Haseo was just another member of that crowd. It was none of his business.

"Ah!" Atoli made a small noise. She'd noticed that Haseo had been watching her. He rebuked himself for not making his escape while he could.

"Haseo." Atoli broke the silence. She walked toward Haseo, smiling as if nothing had changed.

Crap.

"Hi. How is everything?"

That innocence annoyed Ryou. "You're not thinking of everyone else here, making all that noise. This time the PKs are right . . . Moon Tree is always so high and mighty," Ryou criticized her.

Atoli stood there, silent. He couldn't read her player expression. Ryou just got more irritated.

"HASEO!"

"Wha—?"

Atoli's loud shout pierced Ryou's eardrum. He reached for the speaker.

"You don't know anything about Moon Tree. We just want to make the Internet community a better place. We're only thinking of everyone else! We're not preaching. Surely, everyone wants this place to be friendly? Still, we get accused of preaching! I think that people who look down on others, simply don't understand how other people feel. Am I wrong, Haseo?"

Ryou just despaired. Atoli couldn't ponder anything but her own agenda.

"Please!"

YOU RECEIVED ATOLI'S MEMBER ADDRESS!

"What . . . ?"

She had pushed her member address on him. Ryou didn't want this!

"I just want you to understand what Moon Tree is about. I'll explain it all to you."

"I don't want anything to do with it."

"Please let me help you," the voice of the Shadow Warlock, Sakubo, called out from behind Haseo. Evidently, Sakubo had managed to catch up.

In front of him was Atoli. Behind him was Sakubo. Haseo had no chance of escape.

"Is this a friend of yours?"

"My name is Sakubo of Canard. Please call me Bo."

Atoli and Sakubo exchanged greetings. There was then a long silence.

"Okay, this time we all can go adventuring together!"

"Don't decide in private chat. . . ."

The silence obviously had been because they were private messaging each other. Haseo hadn't read their chat, but he had a good idea what had been discussed. One side was Moon Tree, the other was a self-declared Newbie Support Volunteer. They both wanted him.

"I bet they're getting on well," Ryou muttered to himself.

"I know a good area. I know you'll just love it!"

Atoli was now acting like a guide. Haseo wasn't comfortable with having to move at her pace.

Ryou hadn't been walking the wrong road all this time. The reason that Shino was in a coma had something to do with The World. Each step was bringing him closer to the mystery. He had to keep pursuing Tri-Edge, who held the key. To explore The World, he needed to level up. As he was, he couldn't go to any areas populated by monsters.

I have to level up again. . . .

He had to regain the half year that he'd lost. Even if he let go of his beliefs and joined a party, he had to keep hunting Tri-Edge. Atoli was a member of Moon Tree. Even if they were up against the PKs of Kestrel, he imagined the result would be a stalemate. He should use things that he could—including this meddling Newbie Support Volunteer and preacher.

Ryou told himself to think about the pros and cons.

"Hey, you . . ." He spoke to Atoli.

"Yes?"

"I'm weak now. Why haven't you said anything?" Haseo had been at a godlike level in the game. Now he was a level 1, and he was completely different. Ryou sighed at his own limitations.

Atoli turned to look straight at Ryou. "You look different, but you're still Haseo inside, right? Moon Tree members do not discriminate on a player's level." Atoli grinned.

She looks exactly the same. . . .

For an instant, Atoli had looked exactly like Shino, creeping Ryou out.

● ⬡ ●

THREE

△ SUBMISSIVE TRAGEDY'S 1000 OAKS

The area that Atoli had invited him to was a common starter area. It was a night area, where the stars glittered and the constellations shone bright. They drew out stories of the mythology of this world.

"Are you sure I'm not causing you trouble?"

"If you were, I wouldn't have invited you."

Ryou wasn't enjoying this.

Atoli was quiet for a while, but then she came back to herself and continued.

"I really like this area. Tonight's moon is even more beautiful than usual, though."

"More beautiful? It doesn't change. This is a game."

"Well, let's aim for the beast statue! Come with me!"

What a weirdo.

Haseo felt hopeless. But pulling himself together, he equipped his weapon. Adept Rogues had the capacity to use a great number of weapons, but as level 1, Haseo hadn't yet completed the Job Extend, so he could use only the beginner's weapon. For Haseo, this meant only his dual swords. It was like using a letter opener.

"Right . . . so this is the area . . . um . . ." Bo started explaining.

Ryou let him get on with it.

By killing weak monsters with them, Haseo had gained some experience and levels.

"Haseo, heal!"

"I don't have any heal spells!"

"Run!"

But otherwise, Atoli and Bo were useless to him. They left their healing to too late. If they used a spell, they would do it too close to a monster and be interrupted by an attack. To top it off, the balance of the party was all wrong: an Adept Rogue, a Shadow Warlock, and a Harvest Cleric. What should have been a full tank was too low on fuel because their magic user, the Warlock, was a kid. This was why Ryou had become very picky since starting out in The World.

At this rate . . .

This was irritating. It could take months for Haseo to regain his former strength. It was going to take too long.

Raven.

That strange guild. They knew something, Pi and that Yata guy. Their weird modified @HOME . . . and they had Shino's PC. They weren't following the rules. They were as good as magicians in this world.

I've got more important things to do than play with these kids.

Even if he had to cheat, he didn't mind getting his hands dirty now. Ryou had rejected Raven after feeling a deep down disgust for their secret recording of Shino, but he was going to have to shake that off now.

● ⬢ ●

After killing the area's monsters, the party felt they could relax a little as they headed toward the beast statue.

"The origin of the guild name Moon Tree—"

"I'm not interested."

Atoli was going to invite him to their guild. He most definitely didn't want that. Moon Tree members were known to be like religious preachers.

"Moon Tree is divided into seven divisions. Sakaki is a captain of one of those. Do you remember him?"

Sakaki was that long-haired PC who'd been with Atoli before.

"That's the beast statue." Bo pointed.

They'd passed through the gateway, down some stairs, and into an underground room with an altar.

"That's the Item God." Atoli guided him. "There's a treasure chest there. Haseo, you can open it!"

With Atoli and Bo encouraging him, Haseo walked toward the beast statue, targeted the chest, and opened it.

Suddenly, a memory flooded Ryou's mind—from the day that he'd first logged into The World, when Haseo had been killed.

He had been PKed by a player who went after newbies. He heard footsteps behind him now, and Ryou instinctively turned his camera around.

"Wah!"

"A present for Haseo!" Bo made a clapping motion to congratulate Haseo. "Why don't you try equipping it?"

"Okay."

The two anxious PCs watched him, Haseo gave them a cold glance and then equipped the blades he had taken from the chest.

Haseo's graphics changed.

"Wow, looks cool!"

"It suits you!"

Seeing them smile so naively made Ryou laugh with derision. He'd progressed from a letter opener to a pocket knife.

"I want to get back to how I was."

Neither Atoli nor Bo understood what he was saying, and both wore question marks.

"We got what we wanted. Let's go back to the town."

He had been reminded about what it was to have to level up. He couldn't take it anymore. He decided that he was going to have to contact Raven and that woman Pi. He didn't care if he cheated at this point. His goal was to rescue Shino. To control poison, you needed poison. Tri-Edge was an illegal entity, anyway.

Haseo and Bo were just about to step on the platform that would return them to the Root Town when Atoli stopped them.

"Huh?"

Atoli looked like she was searching the area. Ryou was suspicious.

"Huh?"

"Um, Haseo."

"What? I've had enough of looking at the moon."

Atoli was staring up at the moon.

"It's not that. Can you hear anything?"

Atoli was pointing toward the beast statue.

"Hear something . . . ?"

Ryou turned up the volume on his M2D set, but all he could hear was BGM.

"I can't hear anything," he answered Atoli.

Bo couldn't hear anything, either.

"How can that be? I could hear something rustling. It was coming this way."

"Go alone," Haseo refused.

"Haseo, come too!" Atoli was firm.

For some reason, he couldn't turn her down again. He didn't really understand what hold she had over him.

"It's this way!" Atoli called as she ran around to the back of the beast statue. Bo and Haseo followed.

Dadum. Ryou's heart skipped a beat. He was terrified.

"This is it." Atoli touched the wall.

It was there. "The mark of Tri-Edge?!"

On the back of the beast statue, there was the Tri-Edge's mark, flickering.

"Tri-Edge . . . what does that mean?"

"It's glowing . . . red. It's scary," Bo muttered.

Ryou's pulse was racing. It was like a door to another world. For some reason, he remembered something he'd done when he was very young. He'd believed that he could enter the TV, and so he'd try to put his head through the screen.

Then, he was even more amazed.

"How?!"

He could target the symbol.

Typically, the symbol of Tri-Edge was carved into the background, but this one he could select as if it were an object he could interact with.

"I think I can hear something coming from this mark . . . Perhaps it's from the other side of The World?" Atoli sounded curious.

The other side of The World.

Ryou's hand was shaking. As if he were invoking a mysterious power, he pressed the select button.

Aaaaaah! He was forcibly transferred.

● ⬡ ●

FOUR

There was a rush of static. The static slowly faded, and the M2D speakers started relaying the sound of running water.

Ryou hadn't seen this scenery before. It was a cave, but it wasn't one of the ordinary dungeons. On the floor of the cave was a clear lake of water.

"An underground lake . . ."

Bo was looking around. From an island in the middle of the lake, a large tree rose. The trunk and the branches looked like crystals. They appeared so delicate that it seemed they might shatter at the slightest touch.

Haseo checked his map data.

"Dead Wood."

"Is this a Lost Ground?!" Atoli cried with joy.

△HIDDEN FORBIDDEN DEAD WOOD INDIEGLUT LUGH

This was a Lost Ground—Indieglut Lugh. Ryou couldn't tell if that was supposed to be the name of the tree or the lake.

A small amount of light fell onto the cave floor and quiet lake. Where the light hit the tree, it dispersed in a thousand directions. The crystal tree sparkled blue as if it were a newborn star in the universe of this deserted cave. There was no BGM, and the only SFX was the pure splashing of water.

"Wah!"

Atoli and Bo ran toward the lake. You could paddle along the edge up to your ankles of the sandy shore. But it didn't look like you would be able to cross to the island in the middle of the lake that way.

"Hey! Stop messing around!"

A Lost Ground connected to Tri-Edge's sign . . . Ryou was very alert. This wasn't legal in the game. Just like with the attack at Hulle Granz Cathedral, Tri-Edge could appear again.

"But isn't it great? We discovered a Lost Ground!"

Atoli was ecstatic. She played along the lake's edge.

"Hey, there's someone there. . . ."

Ryou looked over. On the island, standing under the tree, was a single PC.

It was a young PC. On top of his long hair, he wore a hat decorated with flowers. And with his light, silver armor, he resembled an elegant imperial guard. His model was probably a Blade Brandier. Unfortunately, he was too far away for Ryou to get his details screen.

"It's a shame we weren't the first ones," Atoli sighed.

"How did he get across, I wonder?"

Bo's question was simple but unanswerable. From where they were standing, the island and lake were part of this area's background scenery—scenery that shouldn't be accessible. Yet there was the youth, standing in the middle of it. The youth, as if an actor on a stage, dramatically raised his hands to the heavens.

A strange effect came from the silver knight's fingers.

"A cat . . . ?"

Black bubbles . . . strange black spots were appearing, tracing the path of his fingertips.

"What is it? It's so pretty," Atoli sighed as she watched the dance of the knight and his black bubbles.

Bo said it first. On the shoulder of the silver knight was what looked like a cat. And every now and then, it looked like it was speaking. Ryou couldn't catch what was being said, though.

"Those spots look like soap bubbles! Is there an item that can do that?" Atoli asked Haseo.

"No."

Ryou couldn't recall any item or spell that involved black spots like that. It was becoming a bit questionable whether this silver knight was indeed a PC. He looked like a fairy from a painting. Ryou was starting to think that it might just be an Event Character or an NPC. The only way to confirm this would be to talk to the silver knight.

"Hey there!" Ryou tried to engage the young man.

However, the silver knight said nothing, instead disappearing in the shade of the tree as if stepping backstage.

"The noise is coming from him," Atoli whispered.

Noise. That's right. When they'd found the sign, Atoli had said she could hear a noise coming from it. Then, they'd been forcibly transferred here. That was how they'd found this Lost Ground, and become witness to this strange silver knight and his cat.

"What the hell is going on?" Ryou asked, without really expecting an answer from his companions.

He was intrigued. He had a feeling that this had something to do with his own search.

Black spots . . . that's . . .

On Shino's PC!

Those black spots had been on the remnants of Shino's PC, which he'd seen at Raven's @HOME.

And Atoli . . . ?

What could Atoli's player hear? For the first time, Ryou had a personal interest in Atoli.

"Let's check it out!" Atoli ran to the water's edge. There didn't seem to be a route to the island, but she started looking for a gap in the invisible wall.

"Get away!" someone shouted. It wasn't Haseo's or Bo's voice.

When Atoli turned around, the texture of the water was breaking up. The lake was exploding!

"Aaah!" Atoli screamed as she collapsed at the water's edge.

"ATOLI!" Bo screamed.

Something was emerging from the lake of Indieglut Lugh, something Ryou had never seen before.

"What?!"

Ryou couldn't believe his eyes. A terrifying creature that looked like a microbe had appeared. It looked like it should be tiny, but it was inflated to a size much larger than a PC. It squirmed and twisted. Ryou instantly recoiled in psychological disgust, and his skin became covered in goose bumps.

The monster's tentacles were secreting the black spots, which now covered the surface of the clear lake, staining it like black oil.

Ryou couldn't target it. This wasn't a monster that you could attack like normal. They could do nothing to it, even though it had leveled Atoli with a single attack.

The black bubbles spread out over the lake and eroded away at the Lost Ground's map. Soon, the black plague reached Ryou's feet.

"OW!" It hurt. His feet stung in real life, as if his heels had met hot coals.

They all started to panic. What was this? Why were they hurting in real life? This was only supposed to be a game.

"GET DOWN!"

Someone was running toward them and jumped in front of Haseo and the others to protect them.

Dadum. Ryou's heart skipped a beat again. This time, it was more violent.

Him too . . .

It was a young PC with blue hair. He stood defiantly against the massive beast.

"Magus!" A lance of light appeared, and the young blue-haired Lord Partizan wielded his weapon, a glowing emerald lance.

The potential power that this weapon could unleash was immense, greater than any rare item could achieve. The Lord Partizan wielded the giant lance that was many times bigger than him with ease, and as he thrust it toward the monster, the lance emitted a dazzling green light.

"HYAAAAAAAAAAAAAAAAAAAAAAAA!"

Ryou couldn't breathe.

As if it were finely tuned to the player, the spear increased in brightness.

What the . . .?

Still, Ryou held his breath.

Finally, the microbe beast reacted to the Lord Partizan's presence. It crawled and squirmed. The monster seemed to dislike the green light.

"The thing that pierces is my will," the young PC chanted. Around his sword, a digital design appeared.

That's . . . Ryou gazed in wonderment. It was the same skill that Tri-Edge had used, the skill that had reduced Haseo to level I. Raven Guild had called it Data Drain. This must be the same!

"Flash of Green!"

Thousands of beams of green light scattered and turned into beautiful darts. Then the beams that shot from the giant lance attacked and pierced the monster. The monster oozed black spots before it disappeared. And the lake returned to silence.

Ryou was dumbfounded. "Who are you?" Ryou asked the Lord Partizan.

"AIDA have infected the data of The World. They can even threaten the player's life." The youth sheathed his giant lance and turned to Haseo.

"AIDA?"

Yata and Pi had spoken of these AIDA before.

"You've heard of them? They're the reason for the Lost Ones. The only players who have the power to defeat them are Epitaph Users."

The Lord Partizan was saying something that Ryou didn't understand. Then Atoli, who had collapsed by the water's edge, spoke.

"Huh? What . . . what happened to me?" She sounded disorientated.

"What?" Haseo asked.

"This monster that came out of the lake attacked me, and there was this huge noise . . . Like it was coming from inside my head."

Ryou hadn't been able to hear that noise. Bo hadn't heard it, either.

"And then it was like my memories just disappeared," Atoli grimaced.

Memories disappeared?

"Did you lose consciousness in the real world?" Ryou probed.

She had lost consciousness for a moment. She'd almost become a Lost One. It was exactly the same as when Tri-Edge had used Data Drain on Haseo.

Ryou recalled what Raven Guild had told him: These were not part of the specifications of The World. No one knew what they were, if they were an event or a phenomenon. This word, AIDA, it referred to Tri-Edge, the black spots, and microbe monsters. All these things belonged to the term AIDA. They could enter into scenery where it shouldn't have been permissible according to the programming. And that silver knight and cat . . . they must have been dangerous, too.

"It doesn't matter now. The important thing is that you're all okay," the Lord Partizan said cheerfully to Atoli.

"Who are you?"

"Me? I'm Kuhn." Kuhn gave Atoli a little wink.

"What was that monster?" Ryou demanded to know.

The monster couldn't be targeted or attacked. That microbe wasn't really part of The World. And the bug that Kuhn used to defeat it was illegal itself probably. What had he called it? Epitaph Users?

"Yeah. Was it a bugged monster? It's dangerous. We shouldn't come here again until CC Corp has cleaned it up," Kuhn smiled.

"You're good at lying," Ryou said to Kuhn.

"Huh?"

"That wasn't just ordinary bugged data. It makes people lose consciousness!"

When they had been forcibly transferred by Tri-Edge's sign, they'd met an illegal monster, and one person had temporarily lost consciousness. This had to be related to Shino's condition.

"I don't think I was unconscious . . . I was just scared and got a bit confused."

Atoli didn't like people fussing over her. It was also in human nature to try and make things out to be less threatening than they actually were. It helped people feel safe. Ryou ignored Atoli and approached Kuhn.

"What is that huge lance you used to defeat the monster?"

"Lance?" Question marks appeared over Atoli and Bo.

"You couldn't see it?"

Atoli might have been unconscious, but Ryou found it strange that Bo hadn't seen it, either.

"It's an Avatar," Kuhn told Haseo to satisfy him.

"Avatar?" In the Internet community, the word avatar was typically used to refer to the characters or images people used to represent themselves online. But when Kuhn said the word, it appeared differently, in kanji instead of Roman letters.

"Yes, Haseo, Terror of Death."

"How do you know me? And that light that came from your lance, it was the same as Tri-Edge's Data Drain!"

"That was the power we Epitaph Users hold." Kuhn smiled enigmatically. He continued as if he could see right inside Ryou's heart. "That lance is my Avatar, Magus."

"Magus?"

"You want to know more? About AIDA, and Avatars, and Epitaph Users?" Kuhn was inviting him.

"What do you know?"

"You can use them, too."

Haseo hadn't expected that answer.

"If you could see my Avatar, then you and your PC have the ability, too. And your ability to be an Epitaph User is starting to awaken. Can you feel it, an unknown power that is hidden in you and your PC?"

Pi from Raven had said something similar, that inside Ryou's PC there was a power hidden.

"Avatar . . . Epitaph User . . ."

"You should be able to feel it. Epitaph Users connect with their PCs on a level that transcends the controller and display."

Kuhn was talking in the same way the Raven members had.

"How can that be possible?"

"You don't believe me?" Kuhn reached out his hand toward Haseo. "I know it doesn't make sense, but you can't deny the real pain and the condition of the Lost Ones."

Ryou had to believe him.

He could remember the burning pain on his feet. The image of Shino laying there in the hospital bed. The pain of the black spots. The agony of Tri-Edge's Data Drain. Ryou was motivated by his desire to save Shino. This was his hope.

"If I have the same power as you, show me how to use it," he commanded Kuhn. Ryou was thirsty for knowledge and power.

"Then come with me." The words held behind them the promise of learning more about Tri-Edge.

Kuhn sent Haseo his member address. He told Haseo he would be in contact, and then he left.

CHAPTER_04 : DEMON PALACE

days later, Ryou received an e-mail from the mysterious PC As he tried to calm himself, he logged into The World.

The meeting place in the e-mail was Ω Server Root Town: a Cloth—The Warring City. The streets were lit up like Las and the architecture here didn't belong to any one particular e. The gaudy neon signs created the feel of a red-light district. This city was the seat of power for Teutates the Pursuers, a mixed force of humans and beasts who were in search of pure power, distinct from good and evil.

"I wasted that jerk!" A large PC and his gang passed alongside Ryou. Lumina Cloth was a big city, but the only place most players visited was the main street.

"The Arena?" Down a long avenue of lit-up palm trees was a foreign-looking building that served as the Arena Hall. Lumina

Cloth was the Root Town for PvP combat areas, and it was the haunt for players who weren't satisfied by killing monsters and so wanted to prove their superiority by taking on other human players. Even the atmosphere here was different from other areas. Here, individual power meant everything.

"Hey, Haseo." A friendly voice called out to Haseo, who was now standing right outside the Arena building. It was the blue-haired Lord Partizan, Kuhn.

"You're late," Haseo grumbled.

"Sorry, got distracted by some pretty ladies."

Ryou couldn't tell if Kuhn was joking or telling the truth. Maybe that was what Kuhn was into. Kuhn always acted cheery, but it seemed false somehow.

In the center of tiered rings of spectator seats that were arranged coliseum-style, a battlefield was marked out with lasers. The ceiling was covered in stars like a planetarium, and hanging from it were multivision screens, making the Arena Hall look like a space station floating in the Milky Way.

Haseo and Kuhn were seated inside the Demon Palace in the spectator section, chatting.

"The Terror of Death has never taken part in the Arena?" Kuhn seemed disbelieving.

"It's just for showing off. I'm not interested in that."

Haseo had been to Lumina Cloth in search of information on Tri-Edge, but he hadn't participated in the Arena.

"Well, PKing and the Arena are very different."

The PvP matches that took place in the Arena were battle events that occurred with the consent of both players. It was a sport, very different from the aggressive preying that PKs enjoyed.

"The Arena has nothing to do with PKing," Kuhn said. "CC Corp created the Arena in an attempt to provide an outlet for the cruel element of the PKs. It was designed as an appropriate place for demonstration of that play style. And they hoped that building the Arena would make The World a safer, more stable place. In the end, though, it just turned into a hangout for the immoral players."

"Oh, so that's why." This was the first Ryou had heard that explanation.

"Haseo, I think you should get to understand The World better," Kuhn giggled.

Looking back, it had been eight months since Ryou had joined The World. For the first two months, he'd been a member of Twilight Brigade and had spent all his time with Ovan and the others. He'd relied on Shino for everything. The guild had been devoted to searching for a mythical item called the Key of the Twilight, so they hadn't followed the roads that normal beginners did, earning money and leveling up. Instead, they were more like wandering seekers of truth. Then, for the past six months of his time in The World, he'd lived the life of a PKK.

Ryou was now a cripple here. He didn't have any knowledge of how normal people played The World, or even how it operated on a day-to-day basis. The same went for the Arena.

"I didn't come here to listen to stories."

"Don't be so hasty."

Kuhn had opened a personal chat box with Haseo. They were going to talk about the Lost Ground, Indieglut Lugh, and the illegal monster they'd encountered there.

"AIDA monster?"

"It's a monster that has been infected by AIDA data," Kuhn replied. "AIDA infect things with data and cause unusual and extreme things to happen. If it's a game monster, it will go into a frenzy and attack PCs."

Haseo hadn't been able to target the microbe they'd encountered. It was like a bugged monster that could attack but couldn't be attacked itself.

"AIDA are viruses on the network?"

"Not quite. They seem to operate in a similar fashion, but PCs that have been attacked by AIDA . . . well, you know what happens."

That was the problem with Shino.

"The attacks on the PC cause real-life pain to the player. . . ."

"And if you were PKed . . ."

Just like the way Atoli had lost consciousness for a while. And like Shino . . . a player could become a Lost One. Was Tri-Edge an AIDA?

"It's like a horror movie."

A virus in an online game could develop in a player like a real-life virus. It was disturbing. These abnormalities were called AIDA. Kuhn and Raven Guild had used the same term.

"You can guess the reason why CC Corp hasn't publicized the existence of AIDA."

Did CC Corp know about AIDA? Ryou didn't know the answer to that. However, Ryou suspected that CC Corp didn't advertise the existence of AIDA because they prioritized company profits. Also, even if there was an uncontrolled problem, it was impossible to prove a link to the game and the coma victims. They could never accuse CC Corp and the AIDA without proof. Ryou's rage toward CC Corp increased.

"Kuhn, why are you after the AIDA?"

"Me?" Kuhn fell silent for a moment. "So that I know I'm doing what's right."

"What's right?"

"To protect players from them. That's why I'm exterminating the AIDA."

"You wanna be a hero?"

"Something like that." Kuhn was shameless. "Because I've awoken to my Avatar's power as an Epitaph User, it's my duty to protect ordinary players from AIDA."

Another movie hero born in The World.

"That lance?"

The Avatar—Magus—was in the form of that giant lance, and it had exterminated the microbe-esque AIDA by Data Drain.

"We're here for the title match at the Demon Hall Arena!" Ryou's questioning was cut off by the yell of a Game Master drawing the Arena's occupants' attention to the center of the battlefield.

"What's going on?" Ryou asked. He didn't understand.

In the middle of the battlefield, a PC transferred in. Lit up by a spotlight was a long-haired Blade Brandier.

Dadum. Ryou's heart skipped a beat again.

Standing in the center of the battlefield were the silver knight and cat that had been in the background scenery of Indieglut Lugh.

"AIDA is infecting PCs." Kuhn's voice sounded tense. He meant . . .

"AIDA . . . PC . . ."

"Yes, he's Emperor Endrance. He's an AIDA-PC."

AIDA-PC. Ryou realized something . . . perhaps that was what Tri-Edge was—an AIDA-PC.

Endrance blew out black spots like bubbles. On his shoulder was the cat. The Emperor was the strongest PC in Demon Hall Arena.

The challenger appeared on the battlefield: a female Twin Blade.

"The competitor is the previous Emperor, Alkaid. She lost her title to Endrance," the commentator continued.

"A revenge match?" Ryou muttered with interest.

Alkaid looked confident; she must have prepared well. She made a pointing motion at Endrance.

"I won't be tricked by you a second time!" she shouted at him.

Endrance had clearly done something to Alkaid in the past. Ryou wondered what she meant by "tricked."

"Tricked?"

"If you watch, you'll see," Kuhn answered.

Ryou watched the battlefield in silence.

Alkaid maintained her pose and didn't move. On the other hand, Endrance stroked his hair back and then, with quick, detailed movements, he started to play with the cat on his shoulder. It was weird. Alkaid's motion commands clearly had been entered via the controller, whereas Endrance managed to look more like an Event Character in a cut scene. Programming such detailed movements wasn't simple. Endrance must have been cheating.

"Data Drain is the power to alter data," Kuhn muttered. He was clearly predicting that this was going to happen here.

"What . . . ?"

"Data Drain itself isn't good or bad. It depends on the person using it as to whether he becomes an angel or a demon."

"What do you know? What's going to happen?" Ryou yelled, enraged.

"Haseo, you must be able to feel it, too. Epitaph Users, like us, connect with their PC in a way that surpasses the controller and display. Likewise, Epitaph Users connect with one another."

Who is us? Kuhn? And Endrance? What's an Epitaph User? Ryou's soul was screaming out. And even his PC, Haseo, was . . .

"Let the fight commence!" a voice bellowed.

"That title is mine!" Alkaid attacked.

Endrance dodged, and Alkaid followed up her attack.

"Huh? He's just running away."

Ryou could hear voices of discontent amongst the spectators in the Arena. Endrance was simply avoiding attacks. His evasion technique was excellent, but that didn't make for an interesting show.

"Endrance always fights like this. First his opponent attacks, then something changes," other spectators explained with knowing looks on their faces.

And then Ryou finally noticed: The impatient, fleeing PC wasn't the champion, but the attacking competitor.

"I can't get a hit. . . ."

Alkaid was just slashing at the air each time.

"This is boring." It must have been Endrance who'd said that. "She'll get bored of this fight."

As soon as that disappointed voice whispered, Endrance started issuing the black spots again.

"You're right, Mia."

Was Mia the name of the cat? It still stood on Endrance's shoulder, and it didn't look like it was going to budge at all when Alkaid unleashed a third attack.

Endrance was talking to the cat. And that was being passed through Haseo to Ryou's M2D.

"Yes."

Ryou watched with interest. Time stopped. Time in the real world kept flowing, but time in The World had stopped. And in Endrance's right hand . . .

"Disappear. You are nothing more than an ugly doll."

Suddenly, time started again. Alkaid should have been right in front of Endrance, but she'd disappeared. The spectators whispered to one another. Finally, the challenger was spotted in a corner of the battlefield: a gray corpse. Her head was drooping, eyes wide open, just like a doll.

The audience fell quiet.

"Instant kill!" The commentator announced. "Emperor Endrance defeats Alkaid in one hit! Some grudge match!"

The silence of the Arena turned to an uproar, and the whole place exploded in excitement. The spectators chanted Endrance's name, celebrating their victorious Emperor.

"What did he do?"

"I've never heard of such a skill."

"High-level fights sure are different. . . ."

In the history of the Arena, there had never been an Emperor as showy and as strong as Endrance. The spectators were gasping at his power. But Haseo had seen the whole thing, and there was an enitrely different reason for his gasp.

"Did he just —?"

"Yes, Endrance used his Avatar." Kuhn's voice was full of tension.

In Endrance's right hand . . . "Avatar."

"The others can't see it."

It wasn't showing in their displays. They couldn't have known why the challenger had lost and why Endrance had won.

However, Ryou had seen it. It showed in his M2D.

"He's the Epitaph User of the Temptress."

Ryou stared at Endrance while Kuhn spoke. In Endrance's hand was a beautiful rapier with a hand guard shaped like a rose. This, too, looked like a weapon that was emitting some sort of illegal force that couldn't be achieved by any rare item.

"That is the Avatar, Macha."

That sword had Data Drained Alkaid and turned her into a lifeless doll.

The show was over, and the audience was leaving.

"The poor player."

"She's not unconscious is she?!" Ryou was looking with dismay at the collapsed Alkaid.

"It's the same as a virus. If you receive an attack by an AIDA, it doesn't necessarily mean that you'll fall unconscious. . . ."

"Why doesn't CC Corp just suspend his account?!" If they would just cancel the contract and suspend his account, then the player Endrance wouldn't be able to login anymore.

"Because they couldn't, even if they wanted to."

"WHAT?!" Ryou was horrified. It meant that AIDA were above the system.

"You're shocked? At Endrance?"

"Yes."

"I see."

"That wasn't a battle. He's a murderer." Ryou then left Kuhn alone in the Arena seats.

Emperor Endrance . . . the power I desire . . . to use Avatars . . . to be an Epitaph User. And he was also an AIDA-PC, like Tri-Edge.

What is The World—it was a game that had some kind of magical ability to take a player's soul—*behind the data that doesn't show in the M2D?*

Tri-Edge, Shino, Raven, Kuhn, Endrance, Epitaph User, Avatar, AIDA, Data Drain . . . He lined up all the words in his head and tried to connect them. He couldn't make sense of them. He didn't know what was right. There was some major point still missing.

He *had* to find the connection. To do this, he needed power. He needed power greater than anyone . . . or anything. . . .

As Haseo left the Arena building, in the corner of his vision, he saw the person who held the key.

"Ovan?!" Ryou couldn't stop himself from calling out.

He had seen the tall PC with the strange left arm in the crowd. Had he been there all along? Had he seen the fight with Endrance?

Ovan turned around, looking at Ryou and smiling. He then turned back around and walked off.

Ryou followed Ovan, who entered one of the alleys in Lumina Cloth and took off running. Haseo's thoughts were Ryou's: He needed to know what Ovan did. He had to be told. However, as he turned the corner, Ryou lost sight of Ovan.

"Where are you? Where did you go?!"

Ryou looked around. There was nothing behind the Arena. All was quiet. He was standing in an alley, at a dead end, so if Ryou had lost sight of Ovan, it meant that Ovan had logged out.

"Hey, you! What are you doing here?" a voice came from behind Haseo.

When Ryou turned around, someone was standing there.

"Bo?"

It was Sakubo from Canard, with whom Ryou had created a party before. However, there was something strange about him.

"Who do you think you are?! I don't know you!"

Bo's voice was different from before. It was simple enough to adjust the voice chat audio settings to make a boy sound like a girl, like some people did when singing karaoke, but why would he go so far as to adopt the speech patterns of the Kansai dialect? This kid had attitude and didn't seem to recognize Haseo.

"You're Bo, right?"

"I'm Saku. You want to meet Master En, too, don't you?! How did you know he uses this exit?"

"Master En?"

Haseo didn't get to finish his question, as the back wall of the Arena lit up—and then the wall erupted into black spots. From the tear in the wall emerged Emporer Endrance. Could this be what AIDA did?

"Master En. Great work! You were amazing today!"

Sakubo—or the young Shadow Warlock called Saku—chased Endrance, looking up to him as if he were some kind of idol. However, Endrance didn't give Saku a second glance and kept walking, a vacant expression in his eyes.

It was strange to look at a PC and feel that it was empty.

"What do you want? You've put Master En in a bad mood," Saku said. "Endrance doesn't like scum like you, so you better go—right, Master En?"

But Ryou ignored Saku's protestations. He stood in front of Endrance.

"What are you?" he asked.

Endrance was handsome and tall, over six foot. A purple hat decorated with roses suited this man, but you would never meet a man like this in real life. The cat on his shoulder was as big as a small squirrel when viewed close up—and from its elongated ears and thin eyes, it seemed somewhat fairylike.

"You were at Indieglut Lugh with the AIDA." Ryou wanted to see if Endrance's player knew what AIDA were. "You used an Avatar in the last fight, didn't you?" Ryou also wanted to see if he knew what Avatars and Epitaph Users were.

Endrance's eyebrow seemed to twitch for a second. It was the only time since Ryou had started talking to him that Endrance's iron mask had dropped.

"Hmph." Endrance reached out to touch Haseo's cheek.

Ryou came out in goose bumps. It was real. He had felt a cold hand TOUCH him.

"Wow. You can see it, too." With a strange gesture, Endrance sighed. He then shared a few hushed whispers with the cat on his shoulder. Haseo couldn't hear this time.

"But you're pathetic. You have no power."

Endrance looked down at Ryou with disdain. Endrance was like an overacting thespian. He didn't behave like a PC in a game.

"Tragic . . . very tragic . . . so very tragic . . ."

"How dare you?!" All the blood rushed to Ryou's head. He was brimming with rage. "Who are you to tell me I have no power?"

"I think I hit the nail on the head. Look at you fume."

"WHAT?!"

"You can see it. You know it. But you don't understand it. Not understanding it is the same as not having it. Powerless."

"I will show you my power. I will defeat you!" Ryou yelled.

Endrance smirked a little. "You have no chance."

Endrance turned to walk away. He swiftly disappeared into the streets of Lumina Cloth, like a street cat adept at stealth.

Ryou couldn't even give chase. His enemy was illegal. It was the same as battling a beast from another world.

"Look what you did! Fool!" Saku laughed at him. "You want to try fighting? Master En will crush you."

"I thought you hated people who looked down on others," Ryou muttered.

"Ah ha ha ha," Saku laughed. "Look in a mirror! Of course people are going to look down at weaklings like you."

Ryou suddenly remembered Haseo's state and felt dismayed at his weakness. If he entered the Arena, it would be an instant kill.

"Crap."

"You want to fight Master En? You'll have to get a title match with him. Then Master En will crush you."

Saku ran off somewhere.

"Title match?" *That* was how Haseo could stand in front of Endrance and get his full attention. But Haseo didn't currently qualify.

TWO

The following day, Ryou was once again contacted by Kuhn.

"You want to know what you have to do to be able to use Avatars?" Kuhn smiled.

"If I have the ability to be an Epitaph User, then I want you to show me how to use it," Ryou said.

As they walked through the streets of Mac Anu, Kuhn smiled broadly. "You think there's going to be some Avatar command function you can use?"

"I'm wrong?" Ryou *had* thought it would be like that.

"I told you already: Epitaph Users connect with their PCs on a level that transcends the controller and display."

"I don't get it. . . ." Was accepted knowledge getting in the way of Ryou's fate? He needed to start thinking outside the box.

"Epitaph Users have to awaken. That's the only path we know."

"Awaken?"

"That's how we describe it when someone finds his ability to become an Epitaph User."

"Kuhn, when and how did you awaken?" Ryou wanted to know what path Kuhn had followed to open his eyes to an Avatar and become an Epitaph User. If he could do the same, then it couldn't be too long before Ryou and Haseo could awaken and use Avatars.

"I can only speak from experience," Kuhn started. "I took an intense emotional shock, and then suddenly it awoke."

"What is *it*?"

"I don't know anything, except that if you stay in contact with me, your chance of awakening increases."

"You pass it on or something."

"Right. You'll become Batman's Robin?" Kuhn giggled.

Ryou wasn't going to be his helper. Kuhn just wasn't a born hero.

"Whatever. I'm not giving up until I've saved Shino." He finally let it out. Even if he were killed, he wasn't going to let her go.

"Shino Nanao? Is she your girlfriend?"

"OF COURSE NOT!" Ryou's reaction was over the top for such a simple question.

"No need to be like that. There's no better reason than for a girl you love."

"You always have a smart answer for everything, don't you?"

"I think it's just being positive."

They crossed the river and through the gate. As always, the fountain plaza at the center of Mac Anu was full of PCs selling wares.

Ryou noticed a single PC sitting in front of the fountain. "Sakubo . . . ?" It was the Shadow Warlock with the crescent hat.

"He was with you before. . . ." Kuhn remembered him, too.

Yesterday, Ryou had spoken to Sakubo in the alley behind the Arena.

Sakubo lifted his head. He'd noticed Haseo, as well.

"Haseo . . ."

The voice, it was the same as the first time he'd met Bo.

Haseo asked him about what had happened the day before, when they'd both met Endrance in the Lumina Cloth alley.

"Yesterday was Saku's turn," Bo answered.

"Saku's turn?"

"Saku is my older sister. Yesterday, she was using this PC."

"You mean that a brother and a sister are sharing a PC?" Kuhn interrupted the conversation.

It seemed that a pair of siblings were using the same account and PC to play The World.

"Saku and Bo makes Sakubo. . . ." Ryou realized.

The sister was Saku. The brother was Bo. Their PC name was therefore Sakubo. Ryou finally put it all together.

"What are you selling?" Kuhn asked and looked in.

"Oh, sorry."

"What?"

"Um . . ." Sakubo desperately wanted to say something but was holding it in.

Looking at the shop menu, all the items were low value and mostly cheap healing items like Health Drinks. They were all priced so low that Bo was most likely running at a loss. In the shop comments was a note: "Only for beginners." It was asking that intermediate players not buy them because they were cheap.

"You're a shop for newbies?" Kuhn asked.

"Yeah."

"That's nice of you," Kuhn said to be kind, but Bo suddenly burst into tears.

"Uwwwaaaaaah!" The voice chat was filled with the sound of a kid crying.

"What . . . ? Did I say something wrong?" Kuhn was panicked.

"Bo, is something wrong?" Ryou asked Bo.

"No one will buy anything from my shop. If they do, then they'll get PKed."

"PKed? What?!" Kuhn couldn't believe it. Haseo made a crouch-down motion and looked Bo in the eyes.

"Tell me."

Bo managed to explain through the tears.

Ryou couldn't believe what he was hearing. "Bullying?"

The other day, when Bo and Atoli had left the area, one of Kestrel Guild's PKs had seen them.

"He's been watching us ever since. When I leave my shop, scary people are there."

"Because you made a party with me?"

They were just finding excuses to fight with Haseo. They were probably buying up all the items, and then they would go after newbies who bought items from Bo's shop, too. The bullying would only escalate.

They go after other people now.

Rage at those despicable PKs welled up inside Ryou. He wanted to take revenge on them for picking on little Bo, who had done nothing wrong. They were only bullying him because of his association with Ryou.

Haseo was a loner. But that didn't mean he could ignore it when innocents were being upset because of him.

"Why didn't you send me a message and tell me?" Haseo asked Bo.

Bo just started crying even more. "Because I didn't want to worry you!"

"If you'd told me, I could have crushed those scum!" Haseo replied.

"I know what to do," Kuhn addressed Haseo. Kuhn must have been able to see that Haseo was starting to fume.

"Kuhn?"

"I'll meet with the Guild Master of Kestrel and sort this out. So, Bo, no need to look so sad, okay?"

Kuhn was kind. Bo managed to calm himself at last.

● ⬢ ●

△ SNEERING FAILING EMPIRE

Kestrel was The World's biggest guild. Its members numbered greater than five thousand. And because it was such a large guild, it had a high rank, granting it the privilege of an Area @HOME. An Area @HOME meant that if you entered the correct three words in the Chaos Gate, you would be taken to a special area dedicated entirely to that guild, an area specially designed by a CC Corp designer.

Kestrel's @HOME was a hostile place. There were rows of derelict pillared buildings, and in the stone was carved a temple that looked like an oriental ruin.

"We didn't come here to fight, so try to stay calm, okay, Haseo?" Kuhn was obviously nervous.

The @HOME that had been used by Twilight Brigade was nothing but small rooms under a city, whereas this place had the appearance of a major city.

"This isn't just a place for guild members to assemble. At the Guild Master's wishes, monsters have been brought here so members can use them to train."

"You know a lot about this place."

"Do you know the Guild Master, Gabi?"

"Nope. What's he like?" Ryou asked.

"You'll find out soon enough," Kuhn replied simply.

Suddenly, the two of them found themselves surrounded.

"Hey there." A serrated blade and shoulder armor . . . the red-haired woman in front of them was Bordeaux, the PK. Negimaru and Grein were standing behind her.

"What would a defector from Kestrel be doing here?"

Ryou glanced at Kuhn. "A Kestrel defector?!"

"Heh heh. You didn't know? Kuhn used to be the Vice Guild Master."

Kuhn ignored Bordeaux's revelation as if it had no significance. "I had problems with the direction the guild was taking and left. It happens all the time." Kuhn glared at Bordeaux. He looked fierce.

"We want you to stop bullying Haseo and his acquaintances." Kuhn was candid. However, these were the PKs of Kestrel. People like this weren't going to drop an argument so easily.

"I don't know anything about bullying, do you?" Bordeaux asked her friends in exaggerated motions.

"Of course not."

"Don't mess with me!" Ryou was ready to explode, but Kuhn stopped him.

"Don't let them get to you. They're looking for a reason to PK you."

Kuhn was right. Ryou had to bite his tongue.

Then, from across the vast area, they heard clapping. From the temple throne, a single PC approached, slowly clapping his hands together. Ryou was stunned into reverence: A Red Lion with a height of over seven feet, he was a beast of a man.

Everyone fell quiet.

After one more exaggerated clap, the Red Lion looked around.

"Huh? There's no more?" He spoke, seeming to have enjoyed the show.

"It's been a long time, Gabi," Kuhn replied.

"Oh! It has been a long time," Gabi grinned, but only briefly. "And who are you again?" Gabi cocked his head.

For a second, Kuhn was at a loss for words.

"Huh? You don't remember me?"

Gabi's face was blank. He acted as if he didn't remember the former Vice Guild Master. He looked curiously at Kuhn.

Kuhn took a moment and then spoke again. "You've always thought you were funny," Kuhn sighed, tears staining his cheeks.

"Really?" Gabi motioned as if he were surprised.

Ryou was feeling increasingly frustrated by this exchange. "Oy! Freako! Your little guildies have been stalking and harassing— CAUSING ME TROUBLE! You're Guild Master. Fix it!"

At this accusation, Gabi looked at Haseo and Bordeaux.

"Those who want to PK should be allowed to. And those who want to PKK should be allowed to do that, too. Everyone should do what they want. That's what The World is, right, Gabi?" Bordeaux said. She was confident that her Guild Master was going to protect her.

"Right." Gabi made another clapping motion.

Bordeaux was spurred on by Gabi's agreement. "Hear that, Haseo?" she said.

However, in the next moment, Gabi's massive blade was pushed against Bordeaux's throat. The atmosphere chilled.

When . . . ?

Ryou hadn't even had a chance to react. In the blink of an eye, Gabi had moved around behind Bordeaux, unsheathed his sword, and targeted her.

Bordeaux swallowed hard.

"But don't bore me like this. If you can't provide an interesting end to your show . . ." Gabi sounded like a hungry carnivore.

Next thing, Gabi returned the sword, and then made a slicing gesture across his own neck.

Gabi was quite enraged at both Bordeaux and Haseo. They had caused a fuss here in Kestrel's headquarters, over what he saw as a petty argument.

"Hey, Haseo! You really like the Shadow Warlock kid that much?" Bordeaux had gone pale, but she was trying to regain her composure.

"What—"

"PKs and PKKs are the same thing—we both like the thrill of the fight."

"Don't make me out to be the same as you!"

"We should sort this out in the Arena," Bordeaux said.

"In the Arena?"

"At the next title match in the Demon Palace. I have the right to take the challenge next."

"What?" Bordeaux was saying that she had the right to fight Emperor Endrance in the next title match.

"I could gamble that right to fight . . . I can do that, can't I, Negimaru?" Bordeaux asked her inferior. Negimaru confirmed that it was possible to transfer that right. The times for title matches were decided by the Emperor, so if the challenger had reasons he or she couldn't attend, it was possible to transfer the right.

"If I fight Endrance . . ." Perhaps that would awaken Haseo's Avatar. "If I win, you promise you'll leave Sakubo alone?"

"No worries." Bordeaux glanced at Gabi darkly. Finally, she seemed to get some strength together. "You have insulted Kestrel. If we lose this, then we will no longer have a place here."

At Bordeaux's words, Grein and Negimaru both were speechless.

"It's decided then?" Gabi said, now back at his throne.

"I'll e-mail you the time of the match. Go, Negimaru and Grein."

Bordeaux had started walking away when Gabi stopped her.

"Bordeaux."

Bordeaux stopped immediately. "What?"

"Beautiful . . . to see you frightened."

Bordeaux seemed uplifted by Gabi's words. "Sir!" Bordeaux replied to her master before leaving the Area @HOME.

Gabi watched her leave and then withdrew himself.

Only Haseo and Kuhn were left now in the wilderness of Kestrel's @HOME.

"You get the feeling that Gabi knows . . . everything, right?"

Gabi seemed to know all about what Bordeaux's gang had been doing. It almost felt like he knew Haseo would come here. It was like he had scripted it all.

"He doesn't look it, but he is very well informed. Otherwise, he wouldn't have been able to maintain his position as Guild Master of five thousand players."

There was no more bargaining to be done now. Kuhn and Ryou left the haunt of Kestrel.

⬢ ⬢ ⬢

THREE

A few days later, Haseo received an e-mail from Bordeaux.

Haseo stood in a room that had been organized by the Arena GM. Ordinarily, battles were organized by individuals using the registration for the Arena; however, this was a special title match, so it was run like a World event, and was open to the public.

"As today's match will determine who will go on to fight the Emperor in the title match, the bout will occur in the main battle arena, where we watched last time. There will be an audience," Kuhn explained as he kept Haseo company in the same room.

"This is going to be a show?"

"Haseo, you have some of your levels back, but . . ."

The battles in The World were much more action-heavy than in your average RPG. Face offs were closer to that of a fighting game—hits, combos, evasion, all those words applied. But both male and female users had reacted negatively to this stylistic change; far fewer players had continued playing with this version of the game, and the fight change was cited as one of the major reasons for the drop-off. To the strong warriors who gathered here, though, that was nothing more than an excuse of the weak.

That's why I'm going to do this.

With skill and strategy, you could overcome differences in level between you and your match. For that reason, some players thought that the battle system in The World R:2 was a success. By improving your weapon, skills, and techniques, you could defeat a player far stronger than yourself.

"But that strategy has its limits. I'll say this now: You cannot win against Bordeaux as you are."

It was forbidden to use healing items in the Arena, so fights were centered around your PC specs.

"Bordeaux wants me."

"You don't think you can win?" Kuhn asked. He must have realized it.

"She wants to publically execute the PKK, the Terror of Death. I'll let her. Then she'll be happy."

Ryou opened Haseo's status menu. All the figures were hopeless. Bordeaux was one of Kestrel's best players and one of the best PKs. Ryou couldn't see a way to win this one.

"Even if you're going to lose, you have to do it."

"It doesn't matter if the Haseo PC is killed. Besides, this isn't the battle I—" A PC appeared at the entrance of the room, cutting off Haseo's speech.

"Bo!"

"Haseo!"

It was Sakubo. Behind him was Atoli.

"It's almost time." Atoli looked agitated.

Haseo looked at Atoli and spoke hateful words. "Are you here to tell me that the Arena is barbaric or something?"

"No, the players in the Arena fight with consent. Sakaki . . . Moon Tree Guild accepts it." Atoli said without hesitation.

"Sakaki said that, did he?" Ryou mocked her. He glared at Atoli. "I listen to no one. I don't have faith in children who just repeat other people's words and pretend they understand."

"Stop it, Haseo," Kuhn chastised.

Kuhn gestured for Atoli not to worry, Haseo was just fired up before the match.

They could hear the murmur of the crowd in the distance.

"Haseo . . ."

"Don't worry, Bo. They won't be bothering you anymore."

At least, they wouldn't if he stayed away from Haseo. Ryou couldn't bring himself to say that, though.

"Haseo!" Atoli raised her voice. "I can talk to Sakaki and ask him to have Moon Tree send a message to Kestrel. If Moon Tree gets involved, even Kestrel won't be able to ignore it."

"Get lost," Ryou snapped. If they didn't get involved with him, they wouldn't get hurt.

"Huh?"

"This is my fight."

Ryou moved Haseo toward his death.

• ◆ ⬡

There wasn't a single space open among the spectators' seats. Bordeaux had published on the forums that today would be the public execution of the PKK, the Terror of Death, and so a ridiculous number of PKs whom Haseo had defeated in the past had come to witness it.

Kuhn, Atoli, and Sakubo all were looking down at the battlefield anxiously.

And in the corner of the seating was Pi, the girl from Raven.

"We're almost ready to start the decider match for who will be challenger to the Emperor!" the commentator yelled from the front of the spectator seats.

"To introduce today's match, we have Kestrel's Guild Master, Gabi!"

The face of the Red Lion, Gabi, appeared on the multivision screens that were hung up above the battlefield. "I anticipate an excellent show."

"Well, then . . . game on!" Attention returned to the GM. "Are the preparations ready for the feast? The challengers are entering the field!"

On one side of the field, a redhead Blade Brandier was transferred in.

"Don't get too close to *her!* This is Kestrel's vicious beauty, a ferocious beast released from captivity!"

Bordeaux played up to the crowd, swinging her sword and yelling that she was going to destroy Haseo. The audience was ecstatic.

"And challenging her is . . ."

On the other side of the battlefield, Haseo made his entrance. The whole place descended into jeers. The majority of the audience had been PKed by Haseo. All were the enemy of the Terror of Death.

"I don't think we need an introduction for the legendary PKK, Haseo!" The voice chat ran over the booing. It was obvious that the crowd was not on his side.

"Bordeaux's in a fine mood today!"

"You came then, Haseo," Bordeaux said arrogantly.

"You too."

"Ha ha ha," Bordeaux snorted. "Your PC and jokes are cold, Haseo." She unsheathed her thorny sword.

Opposing her, Haseo stood with his twin blades.

"Under the stars, two competitors fight for the right to face the Emperor," the commentator called, working the crowd. "COMMENCE!"

Almost instantly, Bordeaux attacked, adeptly lunging forward.

Haseo dodged her first attack, and then he looked to counter in the follow through. Without giving her a chance to react, he struck. Bordeaux's HP decreased.

"A scratch!"

"Huh?!"

Haseo was quickly laying small hit after small hit, slowly chipping away at her HP gauge. After a ten hit combo, Bordeaux countered. Haseo guarded, but he kept hitting wherever possible, looking for the gaps in Bordeaux's play.

Crap . .

Haseo was at a disadvantage. Because he hadn't performed a Job Extend yet, he could use only his Twin Blade. That was adding to the large disparity between them—basic specs, power, speed, level . . . *everything* was against him.

"Ngh?!"

Finally, one of Bordeaux's attacks hit Haseo. Although it was only one hit, it had a huge impact on Haseo's HP gauge.

This is pathetic!

Bordeaux wore a sadistic grin on her face. She was laughing, confident of her victory. "It's karma! The Terror of Death, reduced to a sniveling worm!"

"Ngh!"

"I don't know what bug caused this, but I'm so very grateful! Now I shall wash my hands in your blood. I don't think there could be a better amusement!"

For Bordeaux and the great majority of players, The World was nothing more than an online game. But to Ryou, it was everything. It was a strange hell that had left Shino Nanao lingering on death's door. That was what drove him. Something—someone—irreplaceable.

Ryou Misaki prepared himself for "death."

"Oh my, poor little Haseo. Already had too much? Come on, what's the matter? Say something!" Bordeaux taunted him.

Like a creepy spider, she shuffled up to Haseo, her thorn sword pointed at him.

He had lost. He couldn't win by any means. How would his PC's death occur? If it were up to Ryou, it would end now.

"Scared? I bet you're scared, Haseo. Scared when you think of your pathetic, lifeless body in front of this audience."

"I do not fear death," Haseo answered. "Do as you wish."

He wasn't afraid of a virtual death. Ryou was fighting real death. To Ryou, everything Bordeaux was doing was nothing more than child's play. He wanted to give up. He was tired, and he rejected this "reality." Ryou took his hand from the controller and stood up.

Haseo stood there, stock still, prepared for death.

"I see. I understand. You think that if you let me cut you down, we'll stop bullying you and your little buddies." Bordeaux made a lip-licking motion. She could see right though Haseo's plan.

"What?"

"Ha ha ha! The Terror of Death's gotten old. I'm an evil PK! Did you forget what that means?" Bordeaux was trying to work the crowd again.

"I'll never stop. Even if I cut you down here, I will never leave you nor your friends alone. Cry and scream and beg, I won't care. Because"—she took a breath before finishing her monologue—"I love PKing!"

The audience cried out in agreement.

Ryou had misjudged Bordeaux. He'd been too concerned for Sakubo.

"The more they hurt, the more I enjoy it! I bully and bully and bully and *bully*, until I rid the world of trash like you! I'll keep doing it until I eradicate you! Then you will never return to The World! Ah ha ha!"

Bordeaux's words were like a spider's thread.

"You . . ." Ryou's despair was all encompassing. Bordeaux had become so corrupt; was he supposed to give Shino up for *this* woman?

I can't lose!

His desire to battle grew again.

Ryou's breathing sped up and his pulse began to beat at the same pace as the second hand on the clock.

Dadum.

He could feel the existence of his PC. He could feel Haseo. And Ryou's heart was beating in time to his.

He was connected via something greater than the controller, greater than the display.

It was *will.*

It was a Shino-shaped void in his heart.

"You couldn't protect anyone!"

Haseo couldn't protect anyone? Bordeaux's words cut him like a knife.

She made her final lunge for him.

If I lose, I won't be able to save anyone.

Haseo hadn't saved anyone in The World. Not online or off. Not Sakubo or Shino.

I don't want to be eradicated.

It was then—*dadum*—that Ryou's display went black.

A bug? No. Haseo's vision had been slowly swallowed by the darkness. There was no sound. It was darker than night.

Black . . . and then there . . . there was a hole. Digital emptiness blacker than darkness, and in it was a single PC: Haseo standing alone in the display. Only Haseo.

Nothing was moving. He wasn't falling, but nor was he floating. From that hole, something was slowly crawling.

It wasn't going to stop.

POWER. That which Haseo had hungered for. In no other place would he find it, for it had lain hidden within himself, Ryou Misaki.

His own will was the power he had sought, and he would use the very last of it to save Shino.

● ⬢ ●

"Come on!"

"Huh?"

Bordeaux didn't understand the meaning of the words coming from Haseo's mouth. "Come on . . . come on!"

Haseo cast his eyes upward, toward the spectator seating displayed on the suspended multivision screen. The PKs, the commentating GM, Gabi, Atoli, Sakubo, Kuhn—even Pi from Raven, they were all there.

And . . . so was Endrance.

Endrance, the emperor, was standing in the corner of the arena. All those present were displayed, the view switching from one to another in turn.

The arena was a whole galaxy of purple. And among all those stars, Haseo shone forth his power like a supernova.

"If you want to die so badly . . ." Bordeaux unleashed a killing blow.

At that moment, the image of a man in colored glasses flashed in front of him. Ryou's eyes bulged. *Ovan!*

Their glances crossing through the screen. Ovan had definitely nodded.

"Die!" A thorned sword rained a deadly blow down toward Haseo.

The world blurred, and Haseo's vision warped. Ryou's vision warped, as well. He felt his beloved Shino—not Shino herself, but the twisted Shino-shaped emptiness within him. Only she could truly fill that void.

Ryou's eyes opened. This was what it meant to fill a form with his will. The blade he'd sought was his determination to save Shino. Ryou's consciousness, projected through the emptiness, merged his two selves into a single aspect. His writhing passion smashed the barrier dividing the 'net and the real world, and Ryou's head exploded into whiteness.

I am born anew, he thought.

Impaled by a shot of pain, his power manifested.

A shock ran through the battlefield. Lightning rained down among the crimson stars of the arena, leaving in its wake a fantastic, motionless object.

Was it the waning moon? No, but that which shone forth from the sky of the Demon Palace was like unto the very soul of the crescent moon: a great scythe many times Haseo's height. A jet black design was intricately etched into the curve of its blade, the symbol of Death—the reaper of souls. As its very sharpness dominated its crimson-sparked surroundings, the scythe seemed a true weapon of legend, fit to pierce the hardest of diamonds.

● ⬢ ●

Kuhn surveyed the scene and took a sharp breath. "So, he's awoken!"

Pi had started to adjust her glasses from habit, but paused, still pinching her nose as she stared intently. "His eyes have opened . . . so, this is Haseo's Avatar."

Bo, watching from among the spectators, called out. "He mustn't!"

"Bo?"

"A bitter taste . . . the taste of rusted steel . . ." Sakubo spoke cryptically. And then he screamed. "It tastes of blood . . . you mustn't use the scythe, Haseo!"

● ⬡ ⬡

Haseo stood before the black crescent moon of the scythe's blade.

His own Avatar . . . Ryou understood without being told—after all, had this not been born from the emptiness within his own heart?

"What the . . . what just . . . what happened?!" Bordeaux, who had been thrown back by the falling bolts, stood flustered. The great scythe that had appeared so suddenly in the center of the battlefield was entirely invisible to her, in no way reflected upon her display. Clearly, though, she felt the will aimed at her, and the fear that came to her from that bloodthirsty, invisible power shown in her eyes.

Ryou's power, his anger, had manifested as a murderous blade. Haseo advanced.

Bordeaux, shrinking before this unknowable menace, cowered as if soiling herself as she gave a girl's shrill scream.

This power, alien to The World, was illegal.

"This is . . ." Haseo unthinkingly equipped the power—Skeith, Terror of Death. He instinctively knew its name and its meaning.

Ryou and Haseo had fused together, the power joining them. Ryou was Haseo. Haseo was Ryou.

They'd become one, released from the limitations of the display and controller. The two were linked as though by a mesh woven from nerves of light.

"Aaaaah!" Bordeaux could not see it, but could surely feel its presence, the will aimed toward her that had the murderous intent of a savage beast, promising to crawl from beyond an unseeable, untouchable boundary to consume her flesh.

The seasoned PC turned to papier-mâché in the face of this, her thorned sword as useless as the poorest knife. She could not resist. As though someone had performed magic in front of a real human, Bordeaux stood powerless, a mere girl.

Haseo, though lightheaded, smiled. He was excited—devilishly so.

As if he were an event character in a movie—or even like Endrance—Haseo put on a performance that was overblown, even for a 'net game.

"Be gone!"

A beam of light seared the darkness.

When calm returned to the battlefield, only Haseo still stood on the battlefield.

Bordeaux was dead, her PC head severed, her red hair ashen.

The Avatar Haseo held in his hand, Skeith, was dripping blood from the tip of its blade and glowing softly gray. The great scythe was truly fit for Death.

Only the image of Haseo, reaping the red-haired girl's head as though he had been cutting grass, reflected in the eyes of those watching.

The crowd went wild. A ferocious shower of applause and jeers descended upon the battlefield.

"What was that skill?!"

"Instant death?!"

"It's Endrance all over again!"

The spectators' surprised voices flew forth.

"He did it! He really did it! Haseo is the victor! A miraculous reversal!" the commentating GM, who had momentarily forgotten his job, raised his voice to its utmost. "What on earth could have happened . . . Gabi, as Guild Master of Bordeaux's guild, do you have any comment on this disastrous outcome?"

Gabi slapped his hands together, as if to say, *Is that all?*

"Hmm? Is it over already?"

"Indeed! It was over in the blink of an eye! After this, I can only look forward to the deciding match with Endrance!"

At that, Gabi posed his muscles for effect. "I AM GABI!"

"We all know it!"

One man walked away from the arena alone, turning his back on the lingering commotion that followed the battle. Ovan, with his usual wry smile, spoke. "Welcome to The World."

CHAPTER_05 : EMPTINESS

ONE

After defeating Bordeaux in the deciding match at the Demon Palace Arena, Haseo was automatically returned to the waiting room, where he howled, alone.

Ryou laughed until his shoulders trembled, drunk with joy. "Heh heh heh heh . . . AH HA HA HA HA." He savored the crisp feeling of cutting Bordeaux's precious thread, feeling it in a way that could never have passed through the controller and display.

Skeith. That power would be his now.

The journey to save the comatose Shino . . . Despite having no means of saving her, Ryou had taken up his blade. Having lost everything, still he strove, and—taking the little will he had left—determinedly seized the emptiness in his heart. The Avatar had instantiated in The World, straddling the border of the 'net and the real world. "I am the Epitaph User of the Terror of Death."

Each Epitaph User held a power linking his spirit to his PC. His form held an Avatar within it. When Ryou understood this, Haseo gained that power.

At that moment, Kuhn burst into the waiting room. "Haseo!"

"Hey, Kuhn. Did you see that? I finally got it, my Avatar!"

Kuhn exploded at the triumphant Haseo. "You fool!"

"What . . . ?"

"Do you have any idea how dangerous it is to use an Avatar against a PC opponent?"

Ryou was momentarily taken aback at Kuhn's sheer level of indignation, but he took hold of himself and replied back. "After what Bordeaux did, she deserved to be punished!"

"She deserved it? Ridiculous! Do you realize that if you'd set even one foot wrong, Bordeaux's player might have been left comatose?"

Kuhn explained that, before coming, he had gone to Bordeaux's waiting room. Bordeaux, also having been transferred automatically from the field of battle, had made no reaction for some time, apparently having temporarily lost consciousness.

"Well, she woke up, didn't she? What's the problem?"

"That's hardly the point!"

"What business is it of yours?" Ryou shouted, annoyed. "It was my battle. And that giant black scythe—Skeith, the Terror of Death—is now my Avatar, my power!"

"An Avatar is no mere cheap trick or cheat item!" Kuhn told him. "We Epitaph Users exist apart from the normal systems of

The World. If we use this power indiscriminately, the very rules of the game will be perverted. You must understand this! Unless you find yourself faced with illegal entities such as AIDA, you must not use your Avatar!"

Ryou laughed cynically. "Well, aren't you a goody two shoes? What exactly is the point of having this awesome power if I don't use it as much as I can?"

"Don't you get it? What you're saying sounds no different than the rationalizations cheaters always make."

"I guess so." Ryou signaled his terrible determination to Kuhn. "Even if you call me a cheater, the most hated thing in all The World, whatever anyone says, I *will* use my Avatar when I need to!"

"Haseo!"

"There's someone . . . someone I have to save!"

Their argument reached an impasse.

"You mustn't use your Avatar against a PC, against a player. That's no different from the behavior of the Tri-Edge you hate. An Avatar is truly a power akin to an AIDA!"

Sensing that further argument would be pointless, Kuhn turned his back with this warning: "Kuhn," Ryou asked the Epitaph User of the Propagation, Magus, "then why do you use your Avatar?"

A silence followed. Then, Kuhn answered simply, but with resolve and determination: "For the safety of the players . . . to rid The World of AIDA."

"You use yours for justice then. And I because I must save her . . . there's no right or wrong in that."

At that, Kuhn departed from the room with these words: "I just don't know. Perhaps you weren't cut out to be an Epitaph User after all."

Haseo was alone. Everything that had happened up to that point . . . *And yet nothing has changed,* he thought.

There was no way to tell Ryou and Haseo apart. Only the vector of their fate was different. All that remained was to raise a sail on the mast of will and set out under the dawn breeze. Haseo had been blessed. Thus, yielding to the twisting of his feelings, Ryou traced longingly the Shino-shaped emptiness in his heart—and he became intoxicated by the unnamable power that resulted, welling up from that hole that was like a window to another world.

TWO

For the few days that led up to the title match for the Demon Palace, Ryou was forced to contain the surge of his feelings.

He wanted to hunt, to hunt anything, just to use his Avatar. More than anything, he wanted to try this new power.

The emperor, Endrance—Epitaph User of the Avatar Macha, the Temptress—he was infected by an AIDA. Not only his PC data, but the player himself was displaying signs of instability. And indeed, there could be no more fitting target for Haseo to test his newfound power upon.

In the Arena, Endrance attacked his opponents indiscriminately. What better justification could there be if defeating him also served to prevent another victim from falling into a coma?

Ryou briefly wished that he'd had the chance to prove himself on an AIDA before joining in battle with Endrance. Kuhn had already eliminated a microbelike AIDA at the underground lake of Indieglut Lugh. Haseo would likewise have to eliminate the AIDA that infected Endrance. It would be a defining test on the path to Shino's salvation. However, Kuhn had been in a foul mood after the otherwise excellent battle of the preceding day, and it hardly seemed the time to go to him for advice. At this, Ryou was sick with frustration.

Thus, it may simply have been a whim that caused him to accept Atoli's invitation to go adventuring with her. Put another way, he, having an Avatar, was bored.

"Thanks for agreeing to come today! I want to lay last time's failure to rest, once and for all."

Nonetheless, Ryou regretted accepting the invitation a little when the typically flippant and high-strung Atoli appeared.

"When going on an adventure, it's always important to prepare for the worst! So I prepared this for you." At this, she gave him a healing item.

"Oh. Thanks."

"I got up early this morning to get it ready. I guess it's kind of like preparing a picnic!"

Ryou thought once more, with some amount of pain, that she was not merely acting; unfortunately, she was genuinely weird. He was strangely relieved at the thought that he was at least conscious of how warped his own thinking was.

"Haseo, let's go!"

"Take a good look at the map. If there's an item statue, it should be this way."

"Never mind that! We'll go this way."

They continued, inevitably at Atoli's pace.

Even with an Avatar, searching The World required a suitable level, and there was no getting away from the fact that Haseo was still a low-level Adept Rogue. Previously, when he had let loose Skeith's skill—Data Drain—against ordinary monsters, Ryou had been punished with a terrible sense of fatigue. The power of Epitaph Users linked them spiritually with their PCs, but it seemed that this power was not inexhaustible.

Under a clear blue sky, Haseo forayed on through the area with Atoli. The balance of their party was as skewed as ever, and Atoli's player level was, as usual, too low—but Haseo's basics were good, and between them, they defeated the monsters with little difficulty. Who exactly was helping to raise whose level was unclear.

"This area is number thirty-nine on my list of favorite spots."

"Thirty-nine?"

"Yes. I have more than two hundred in The World, and I keep adding more. I hope I can show them all to you, Haseo."

"Ha ha."

Weird girl. *It might be catching if you let her into your head too much,* Ryou thought to himself.

Thus they continued, wandering aimlessly under Atoli's guidance. They passed through the unremarkable scenery, Atoli introducing the lucky animals they encountered and the bonuses that could be gained from them while showing him all sorts of "cool stuff." Not for the first time, Ryou wondered just what it was he was doing.

Even though he knew he had to put up with it for the sake of earning XP, Atoli was only playing. She was sitting in her air-conditioned room and having a good time playing a network game, smugly and hypocritically relying on the support of the group called Moon Tree, while at this very moment, Shino was laying in her cold bed in the hospital, unable even to speak.

"Can you see it, Haseo? Over there!"

He looked in the direction Atoli was pointing. In the distance, far across the sea, a giant artifact shimmered like a mirage.

"Apparently it's called 'the Crest Gun.' In ancient times, people focused the power of the Goddess of Light, who was sealed in Hulle Granz Cathedral, and used it to sear away all the gods in the heavens—proof of what happens when fools have power."

"Your view of the game world, I guess," Ryou answered off the cuff, uninterested.

"True . . . but both you and I are spending our time together here in The World. We're living here in The World."

"Living?"

Atoli laughed. "What I mean is that just because we're in a 'net game doesn't mean we should forget about appreciation or companionship."

She gathered some flowers and presented these trifling gift items to Haseo. "Have you ever met anyone here in The World who changed your whole way of life?"

Atoli's face sprang to mind, but in the back of Ryou's mind, the shadow of Shino was ever present.

"Sakaki of Moon Tree is such a person to me," Atoli confessed. "I hate thinking only of myself, just looking for ways to rack up my statistics. Don't you think it's a waste to just charge on through when there's so much interesting stuff to see?"

She paused for breath before continuing. "Do you like to beat people, Haseo?"

"Well, who doesn't?" Ryou replied.

Atoli looked down sadly. "I don't. Really, I've never beaten anyone. I guess it makes me understand the pain of people who can only lose. Being beaten hurts, and I don't like that . . . but, the idea of beating someone and hurting him in the same way is worse."

Ryou let loose the words that he had been holding back. "So that's why you hate PKs and PKKs."

"It isn't just PKs! Always trying to raise your level over other people, always searching for stronger weapons . . . where does it end? When you spend all your time showing off your power beating up people, how can you meet anyone?"

"It's natural to want to become stronger in an RPG," Haseo replied.

On hearing this, Atoli stood up and moved in front of Haseo, speaking forcefully. "Haseo, that only *seems* like the goal. You should stop and look at the flowers at your feet, and the beauty of the scenery. Try to enjoy the encounters you have in The World more!"

"Encounters?"

"Yes!"

"Stop and look, you say?" Ryou chuckled. Then, a laugh welled up from deep within him and would not stop.

"What ?"

"Are you STUPID?"

Ryou's words cut her like a knife. Atoli froze.

"This is just junk!" He targeted the shrubs and flowers around them as he poured this thought into the emptiness in his heart. Drawing Skeith, he lay into the surroundings, venting his irritation.

"Junk! Junk! Junk!" In the face of Data Drain, the flowers transformed and vanished. Atoli was speechless. Even with the Avatar invisible, she had clearly seen the reaping of the flowers.

With the last of the flowers gone, the Avatar vanished, its appetite seemingly sated. "Do you get it now? All of this is nothing more than CG data, polygons, and textures. It's all just an illusion. Just what is so beautiful about this fake world?"

"Haseo," Atoli's voice trembled, but Haseo barked on.

"The one and only real thing in The World is the players! What is so wrong with us testing one another in battle? What is so bad about improving ourselves so that we can become stronger?"

Ryou called out, his voice cold, "Atoli, I can't trust a mere kid, mouthing other people's words that she only pretends to understand."

He felt a terrible irritation toward this girl Atoli, who could rely only upon Moon Tree and Sakaki, and the pretty, powerless words they spouted. It was envy, perhaps, that she was so well protected.

"Haseo, you're strong." Atoli, so confident until now, became suddenly contrite, lowering her voice to that of a shy young girl. "I can't survive like that . . . I have to belong to a guild, or something like that"

Who did that "I" refer to? Surely, it was Atoli's player herself.

Atoli spoke uncertainly, staring at the remaining flowers in her hand. "I just can't deal with the real world. School is just awful. It's like everyone ignores me . . . or like I just don't exist."

She was baring herself to him, clearly seeking sympathy. So she hid herself in the shell of the 'net, able to show her vulnerability in a way that didn't involve getting hurt.

"But . . . if there's someone I can respect, someone who will notice me, I can manage somehow. I have nothing but the 'net. This is the only place I can really be myself."

Her account had the edge of a plea to it, but whatever problems Atoli might be harboring in the real world, and however serious they were, Ryou had no intention of getting involved.

"What? Are you hitting on me?"

"Huh?" Atoli stopped, unable to comprehend Haseo's words.

"First, you're hanging around with me, and now you tell me all this. Are you saying you want to meet in the real world?" He had essentially accused her of using the 'net in search of a relationship.

At some length, Atoli responded hesitatingly. "I didn't mean . . . even if we met in the real world, you'd never like me. You'd be bored being with me."

Even in this pathetic state, she was still looking for sympathy.

"What do you want?" If he could have spit, he would have. His distaste welled up within him. "Do you think you can get a guy's interest, showing your weakness like that?"

What did she want, for him to promise to do anything he could to help her?

"I didn't . . ." Atoli stood riveted to the spot, looking as though the blood had drained out of her. She had no ready answer, and it seemed she could not think of one on her own.

"Just what is it that's precious to you? Appreciation? Companionship?" Haseo spread his arms to show his exasperation.

"I meant—"

"Why should I have anything to do with the likes of you?" Ryou thought that the last thing he should do was show her either appreciation or companionship, and talking further would only increase his bitterness. He gave her no chance to reply.

"Go home." Haseo brushed her off.

"Wha—?"

"I can't deal with you anymore. Stay away from me from now on."

Upon hearing Haseo's words, Atoli stood speechless, as if drained of all power. The bitter silence was torture for the young Harvest Cleric. After a seemingly interminable pause, she said, "I've got a message . . . from Sakaki."

Apparently, Sakaki had initiated a one-on-one chat. Ryou was unsure whether this was true or merely an excuse.

"I'm sorry." Atoli left the area as if fleeing. Her voice betrayed her tears.

In front of his display, Ryou grimaced. "Why would she want me?" he said to himself.

"I lost everything . . . my history, Shino . . . Why would she want me?"

He was consumed with guilt. Now *he* was the one lecturing other people. It hadn't mattered who the person was.

His heart was torn between self-hatred and self-affirmation. "Should I stop thinking about Shino? Quit being a PKK? You don't know a thing! It's none of your damn business!" he exploded at the absent Atoli.

Having lost Shino, he wandered The World alone. And as if that weren't bad enough, the one hundred thirty-three levels he'd fought so hard for had been taken from him in one single instant.

"Am I the one who wants to rely on someone, who wants someone to console me?" It was as if he had wanted to steal, in turn, what had been taken from him.

Ryou truly had wanted to be comforted. Why did Atoli have to come to him then, to want him? She didn't know anything.

"If you don't want anything, they can't take anything away from you." And yet . . .

He wanted only one thing. Only *her* smile would hold any comfort for him. "Shino . . . I miss you."

Only when he had pushed away this pretend Shino had he finally felt her, even if it was only her absence, only the Shino-shaped void in his heart.

● ⬡ ●

THREE

Not many people knew of Raven.

To most players, it was just a useless phantom guild that never really did anything. Even the players who prided themselves on knowing anything and everything about The World knew very little about Raven's goings-on. And if anyone ever asked a Raven guild member about it, the guild was explained away as a Magic Society.

Raven was like a dodgy underground part of The World, unknown to the masses and a frequent subject of rumors. And in the back of that mystery guild lay the Serpent of Lore.

An uroboros circled slowly upon the black wall—the eternally revolving image of a serpent biting its own tail. From the centerpiece extended many branches, every one working together to record all movement throughout The World.

At that moment, on the platform before the Serpent of Lore stood Raven's Guild Master, Yata, a Macabre Dancer whose attire was reminiscent of a Buddhist monk's garb. In the tone of one chanting a Buddhist sutra, he said, "We must contact him."

"Contact him?" The second speaker was the Tribal Grappler, Pi, adjusting her glasses as usual. None were present but her and Yata. "Endrance is a character shrouded in mystery. Even the Serpent of Lore cannot track an AIDA-PC. And searching through all the logs would be pointless."

When Yata laid his hand on the orb controlling the Serpent of Lore, multiple windows popped up, all showing Endrance. Some displayed him battling at the Arena. Others showed him playing with that cat at Indieglut Lugh. "Endrance's past, his abilities as an Epitaph User, his connection to AIDA . . . all unknown."

"What if we have Haseo extract information from him in the Arena?"

"Interesting."

"Would he comply? Perhaps we were too quick to show him what was left of Shino. . . . In any case, do you believe Endrance would be truthful to Haseo?"

"I'll decide what is true and what is false," Yata declared. "Information is not simply carried through words."

"Understood."

"Endrance is, at first glance, a very laidback person. He hasn't logged out once in these past months, although naturally his player cannot have remained awake this whole time. He also dislikes battling and chatting."

"So . . . a recluse?"

"Yes, according to his real-world information. He seems to have but one single vice—the Arena."

Meaning that their chance to discover more about the player behind Endrance and his motives was . . . "The Demon Palace title match?"

"Precisely. Endrance carries the sixth Phase, the Temptress, within his PC. And to ascertain his connection with the AIDA infecting him, we need a third person—preferably a strong one."

"You mean pitting him against Haseo, the Terror of Death?" Pi again adjusted her glasses out of habit. When forcing two particles to accelerate and crash into each other, the result would be a tremendous release of energy.

"Due to the incident regarding Shino Nanao, Haseo has no plan to run away. Their circumstances may be different, but both Haseo and Endrance have a vested interest in staying within The World."

"Like two dark stars that only shine while online . . ."

"You must admit the outcome of this fight will be most interesting," Yata mused. To him, the fight between Haseo and Endrance was merely an experiment, and a study into AIDA.

The serpent continued to encircle itself, devouring its own tail as the Serpent of Lore continued to fill its logs. And Yata, controlling it, was like Odin having drunk from Mimir's spring, imbued with infinite wisdom.

● ⬢ ●

Endrance was at the back of the Demon Palace Arena awaiting his match, pacing back and forth. His slow movements were reminiscent of an unsettled ghost, one you could see despite knowing it couldn't possibly exist.

Whether in the real world or online, Endrance was now walking the thin line between fantasy and reality.

"That Haseo's such a drag, isn't he, Master En?" a small Warlock's voice pierced the tense air. The voice belonged to Sakubo, and its confidence identified the owner as Saku.

Saku went on. "As far as the Arena goes, he's barely out of diapers. And yet he's challenging the great Master En? What a pain! But don't worry. I'll help you handle him!"

"Hey."

"Yes, Master En? What can I do?" Saku was thrilled to have her Prince Charming speak to her.

"Why are you so afraid of Haseo?" Endrance asked.

Saku balked. "L-like I'd ever be scared of a loser like him!"

Upon hearing this, both Endrance and his cat tilted their heads. "You think I'm going to lose?"

"What? There's no way anyone can beat you!"

"Then keep your interfering hands to yourself." Endrance walked toward the wall and disappeared through a black bubblelike gate.

Saku was left alone, staring. "But if I don't do anything . . ." She had a desperate edge to her voice now, despite talking more to herself than anyone. "If I don't do anything, how can I ever get you to like me? Why do I even exist?"

FOUR

It was finally here. The day of the long-awaited title match, the Demon Palace Tournament.

Haseo was impatiently biding his time in the waiting room.

Looks like things are back to themselves for me. Nobody had come to see him before his fight—not Kuhn, nor Atoli, nor Sakubo. And of course, Ovan hadn't come.

Fine by me. I'm a lone wolf, anyway. Always have been.

Ryou attempted to talk himself over it. He was after Tri-Edge, after the one who had PKed Shino. He was the Terror of Death, fighting alone—now and always.

And the inevitable fight was coming. He knew it.

There was a high chance that Tri-Edge was an AIDA-PC. And Haseo was about to face another AIDA-PC, Endrance. He had to win. There was no other option.

If I can't win this, then I can't save anyone.

He had his Avatar now, a weapon to face his enemies with—a blade only Ryou and Haseo could wield.

"Excuse me." The voice came from a Blade wearing traditional Japanese clothing. It was Sakaki of Moon Tree, of all people, accompanied by another young man.

Haseo had nothing to say.

"Oh, *clearly* I got the wrong person."

Ryou knew exactly what Sakaki meant. He was comparing the fully Job-Extended demon Haseo from before with the young-looking beginner level I Iaseo PC that was there now. But Ryou paid no heed to Sakaki's petty remarks. Sakaki was nothing underneath that arrogant exterior, just a busybody know-it-all.

"I heard about the incident with Kestrel. Shocking indeed. I'm sure we'd be more than willing to help if you required our assistance."

"Whose assistance? Moon Tree's?" Haseo scoffed, injecting heavy doses of his own sarcasm. "As much as I appreciate the offer, I don't want to be brainwashed."

"Who the hell do you think you are, talking to Sakaki like that?" Sakaki's partner flared up.

"Relax, Matsu," Sakaki said. So his partner was called Matsu. Sakaki and Matsu . . . like all seven council members of Moon Tree, these two had taken Japanese trees for their character names.

"But he's dragging Moon Tree's name through the mud!" Matsu protested

Sakaki continued on, ignoring Matsu. "Haseo, taking the path of virtue is an excellent choice. But have some consideration for the people you walk that path with."

"And that's supposed to mean what, exactly?" Ryou demanded.

"You said some rather hurtful things. Atoli is a mess."

Atoli. It was clearly too much to ask to forget that she had ever existed.

"Besides what you said to her, there was one other thing: She wasn't very clear about it, but she mentioned something about passing out when she was in a party with you."

"Listen, she was the one following me around. And if you're so concerned about her, then tell her she shouldn't be so damn nosy."

"You are simply incorrigible," Sakaki sighed. "Haseo, I have one thing to tell you: You cannot live your life paranoid that everyone you meet is out to get you somehow. Both in the real world and online, it's better to get to know people."

It was then that the GM appeared to summon Haseo, who stood up to go.

"Get to know people? I don't care about people who rely on common sense at every turn. Because I have a power that transcends any kind of common sense."

Haseo then turned away from the two Moon Tree members and headed for the Arena . . . and the battle of a lifetime.

● ⬡ ●

The crowd was packed at the Demon Palace Arena.

"Welcome, ladies and gentlemen, to the coveted title match of our Arena! Let's greet our contestants, shall we?"

The crowd roared in response.

"The man who has danced through fight after fight since his debut with an undefeated record, Endrance! People far and wide know of his great strength, although his profile and anything personal about him remains shrouded in mystery. With his fascinating appearances drawing in huge audiences, I'm surprised his fan clubs don't have fan clubs!

"And facing him today is a relatively new face to our Arena, Haseo! Despite this being his first venture into the Arena, he's already taken down the fearsome Bordeaux to claim the title challenge. With the same instant-kill skill as Endrance and an amazing ability to turn the tables on any opponent, will Haseo's challenge upset Endrance's perfect record?"

Half the audience consisted of hooting and cheering rogue characters, and the other half was entirely female—all fans of Endrance. He even had his own fan group within The World's community.

"We'd planned to have our opening speech delivered by none other than Alkaid, but it appears she's running late. Please bear with us."

Thus the fanfares began, and the main screen flashed on, with a massive view of the battlefield. As Haseo appeared alone on one of the pedestals looking over the battlefield, he was greeted not by cheers, but by loud booing from the audience, both from PKs and from Endrance's fans. They all wanted Endrance to crush Haseo.

But when Endrance made his appearance, the crowd almost instantly went silent. Not a word penetrated the thick atmosphere of the Arena. It was as if Endrance had cast a spell over the audience. All of them were completely enthralled by his presence, and had seemingly forgotten how to move or to speak.

Endrance reached up and casually flicked his hair, an action not programmed within the game. He was definitely not your ordinary character.

"You can boo all you want," Ryou muttered, eyeing the audience. "You won't be so loud for long."

The group of screens floating in midair were displaying a run-through of the crowd now. Kuhn was there, as was that Pi woman from Raven.

That pink woman . . .

As Ryou gazed at the screen as if looking for something, a voice interrupted him. "So you're here, Haseo." It was Endrance.

"Like I said. I'm gonna prove my power by taking you out," Haseo replied matter-of-factly.

Haseo then switched all his focus to the fight. To him, this fight was a practice run for the other AIDA-PC out there, Tri-Edge.

Endrance just looked at his cat and shook his head sadly.

The battlefield was red. It was time for Haseo to confront Endrance. "What do you know about Tri-Edge?" It was starting to become a stock phrase of his by now.

AIDA were a great unknown, but as fellow AIDA-PCs, there was always a chance that Endrance and Tri-Edge had some sort of connection.

"Doesn't matter," Endrance said apathetically. Looking at him, you could swear that he'd already put the world behind him, along with any ambitions he might have had.

"I'll either end up a Lost One," Haseo said half to himself, "or I'll take you and that AIDA of yours out."

The battle was set now. No running away, no interruptions. Defeat meant death. Just like with Shino.

"Don't bother," Endrance said. "She won't let me lose."

"She?"

The main screen flicked to the commentators' seats. Haseo glanced at who was sitting there—and almost had a heart attack.

"What? Who are you?" the GM spoke up, but he was ignored as the commentator took his seat. It was Ovan. And he had the same mysterious half smile on his face as always.

"Actually, Alkaid should be doing the commentating today," the GM protested.

"Something came up and she couldn't make it," Ovan informed him. "I'll be taking her place."

Remaining supremely unperturbed by the currently very perturbed GM, Ovan took his seat.

The GM looked at Oven timidly and spoke up. "So, do you know either of the participants?"

"The challenger and I were once members of the same guild," Ovan replied briefly.

"Oh! What was the name of the guild?"

"Twilight Brigade."

"Twilight Brigade? That does sound familiar. . . ."

"It was more than half a year ago."

Ryou was staring at the main screen, unable to keep his eyes off Ovan. *What's he doing here?*

He'd met Ovan eight months ago, after he'd first logged in as Haseo and run into the newbie hunters. Half a year ago, Tri-Edge had PKed Shino and thrown her into a coma, and Ovan had disappeared.

The Key of the Twilight . . . the item that Ovan and, by extension, the Brigade had been searching for was a legendary item that couldn't possibly exist. They said that whoever came into possession of it could make all their dreams come true within The World. The Brigade was a treasure-hunting guild, although they were also discovering Lost Grounds for a time.

But after Ovan's disappearance, the guild had broken up. The Key of the Twilight was never found, and they never found out what Ovan had wanted with it.

"Tonight, these two champions clash in the battlefield! Tonight, the meaning of a champion becomes clear to all! Now, challenger, how will you battle the reigning emperor?" The GM raised his voice even louder. "Let the battle commence!"

● ⬢ ●

In Raven's @Home, Yata was also watching the proceedings at the Serpent of Lore.

"'Something came up'? I wonder, Ovan, did you have something to do with that?"

Yata looked at the commentator's seat and smiled a little. Then he directed his gaze toward the fight. The information window of the Serpent of Lore was showing the fight between Haseo and Endrance in real time.

"It seems that AIDA have an interest in the hearts of players," Yata muttered to himself.

Haseo was constantly on the attack, but Endrance was like a ghost, swaying back and forth, dodging his attacks. Haseo couldn't get a single hit in, and he was getting frustrated.

"Is this why it had to happen in the Arena, with everyone watching?" Pi was on the other side, engaged in a private chat with Yata.

"Hostility, malice, and ambition"—one window was showing Ovan in the commentator's seat; he looked up, as if seeing the invisible camera, and gave a faint smile to himself—"this can only improve Haseo's ability as an Epitaph User."

It was a private message, directed at Yata. The Serpent of Lore and the Arena were two completely different areas, so this "chat" felt almost like telepathy.

"Are you saying that our goals are the same?" Yata replied.

"Aren't they, Yata?"

Yata returned to watching Haseo. "AIDA are drawn to Epitaphs."

"And the Epitaph Users are drawn together."

● ⬡ ●

Haseo adopted a different style: staying at mid-range and making quick hit-and-run maneuvers. Despite this, Endrance had yet to draw his weapon—neither his Avatar nor a more ordinary weapon.

"This fight will not please her, not at all," Endrance said.

"Her?" Haseo asked while using a spell. The spell created magical arrows that flew at Endrance, but every single one snapped.

It wasn't that the spell failed; none of Haseo's attacks would hit their mark when he targeted Endrance. Endrance was a bug monster and an AIDA-PC, so no attacks could defeat him normally.

"Well, Mia? What should we do?" Endrance whispered to the cat on his shoulder. The cat mewed and whispered something. Endrance was fighting for the cat . . . "her."

Endrance nodded at his cat. "I will let you hear him scream for his life."

Thus, Endrance summoned his Avatar. Rose petals bloomed and swirled around him, turning into a sharp, deadly blade—the Temptress, Macha.

"Bewitching Wind!"

Endrance's Avatar was surrounded by a rose tornado. Rose petals spun around him at top speed, each one a deadly blade. As they cut into Haseo, Ryou cried out, feeling his character's pain. It felt like his entire nervous system was going through a blender. Haseo was thrown to the floor of the battlefield, writhing in pain.

"Another instant kill! Even the Terror of Death cannot come close to Endrance's skill!" The GM's voice sounded miles away. None of the regular players in the audience could see the Avatars or their techniques.

Dadum. "Never again . . ."

Endrance glanced down, nonplussed.

"I'm not going to lose! Never again!"

Haseo could barely see for the pain. But the pain was stoking him. It stoked Haseo *and* Ryou Misaki. It meant that he was touching The World. He was facing an enemy from the same mold as the one that had made Shino comatose. The pain made him both happy and furious, and served as a strong reminder of the hole in his heart.

"I swear I'll give you enough of a nightmare to make your life a living hell!"

"Bolt of Love!" Endrance brandished his sword and suddenly, on the battlefield, roses began to grow. Their thorns pierced through Haseo, making Ryou feel as if a thousand needles were being jammed into him.

"I'm . . ." *Dadum.* "I'm . . . right here!"

With power exploding from inside him, Haseo let out a great bestial roar. Filling the hole in his heart, creeping from the depths of the darkest ocean, was the Terror of Death, Skeith, a scythe crafted from darkness, shining like silver in the night sky.

Haseo's Avatar came forth, deadly and ready. And now, both Terrors of Death were ready to bear down upon Endrance.

"So, it has awoken."

The Terror of Death, Skeith.

Yata and Ovan both took sharp breaths.

"Haseo's Avatar, it's clearer than before," Kuhn observed, looking over the weapon that very few in the audience could see.

Haseo and Endrance faced off.

"Why are they just standing there?"

"Maybe it's lagging?"

"Come on, fight already!"

All the audience could see was two fighters standing and staring at each other, seemingly haven given up battling.

"The Epitaphs within both their PCs are resonating, causing Haseo's Avatar to awaken." Ovan continued to look up at the empty sky, talking to the absent Yata. "Why has CC Corp allowed Endrance to come this far? AIDA-PCs are the source of the Lost Ones, are they not?"

On the battlefield, Endrance's expression wordlessly changed into a glare at Haseo.

"Even the System Administrators cannot restrict the account of an AIDA-PC." Ovan was holding a mysterious capsule in his right hand and turning it over and over. "So from the admins' point of view, Endrance is Lost. The audience is looking at what is, for all intents and purposes, a ghost."

"A ghost . . ."

"Yata?" Pi couldn't hear anything Ovan was saying. She queried Yata again, but he was entirely engrossed in his conversation with Ovan.

"My aim is to reveal the true nature of those ghosts."

Yata and Ovan were competing in a battle of wits. The information window in front of them was centered on one person: Haseo.

"Now, Terror of Death, fight! Show me a battle between Epitaph Users! The first ever fight between weapons forged from your spirits!"

As the cat on Endrance's shoulder stared at Haseo, its eyes widened.

"Oh, do you like him?" Endrance asked the cat, a little perturbed. "No, no, Mia, look at me!"

Endrance's eyes, overflowing with black jealousy, turned to Haseo with a hateful look. "Now you've done it! You can just die!"

Endrance pointed his sword at Haseo and lunged, stabbing right through Haseo . . . through Ryou.

"Just die!"

Macha cried out, like a glacier rumbling down a mountain. The icy sword blazed with the reflection of dazzling crimson stars as Endrance plunged it into Haseo's prone form. Rose petals flew around like blood, and the battlefield was engulfed in a crimson fog.

"What's happening?"

"Is he attacking Haseo?"

The crowd was astir. They couldn't see what was happening or know what was going on: attacks that were not just wearing on the characters' HP, but on their players' very lives. Endrance was like a tumor that spread pain everywhere.

Haseo had been stabbed through the chest by Endrance's chilly murderous rage. Any normal person's heart would have stopped.

"No . . . at this rate, Haseo's player will . . ." Pi put her hand over her mouth. The Avatar linked a character and the soul of the player. Being attacked by an AIDA-PC or an Avatar could cause irreparable damage to the player. The Data Drain was all about power.

"You have no power. Even though you've awakened it, you cannot use it." Endrance was taunting Haseo now, like a matador about to deal the last blow to a wounded bull. "Now, let's end this."

Endrance took his distance and aimed his sword at Haseo's heart. The Data Drain would destroy Haseo's body, and possibly even end Ryou's life.

"Bewitching Wind!"

But Haseo, to Endrance's shock, stopped the attack dead in its tracks with his bare hands. Such an action was not programmed into The World's battle styles, and Haseo had no such skill following his return to his weaker character model. It was an illegal ability.

"You little worm." Haseo's voice was strong and brutal.

Ryou's thoughts, feelings, will . . . it was all inside Haseo now. The player and character were now in complete synchronization, beyond the use of a display or controller. Ryou had taken Haseo's form and was now directly inside The World.

"Now you'll see what you get for screwing with me!"

A flash, and Endrance's face was contorted in pain for the first time ever. The great dealer of pain was now its victim, in The World and in the Arena where he was supposed to be undefeatable. A thin line of blood began to slide down his cheek.

"Oh, does it hurt?" Haseo roared. "This is pain! This is real pain!" And he leaned his head back and laughed cruelly.

Endrance had been reduced to this by the same power he had wielded, an Avatar—a scythe, formed of pure condensed darkness. "My Skeith!" He raised his Avatar, his power, to the stars—the power borne of the hole in his heart, the illegal power that united player and character. It was all his.

"Skeith, I see it now. You are me. And I am the Epitaph User, the Terror of Death."

"What?"

The cat was licking at the blood on Endrance's cheek. Did it taste of rage, or of fear?

"This is the power of Haseo!" The light of Death appeared in Haseo's eyes, and the scythe was the weapon of Death. What had been the mutual battlefield was now Haseo's hunting ground. Now it was his turn to taunt Endrance, to mock the undefeated champion.

Endrance was frantic now. "No, I don't want to be hurt! Mia, why? I was supposed to be invincible! With this power of ours, nothing in The World should've been able to hurt me!"

"Well, time to prove you wrong."

"Did Mia lie to me?"

Haseo put on the visage of a demon and swung his scythe. "I will save Shino!"

And blood flew everywhere.

The battlefield disappeared, and all Ryou saw was a blinding flash. And then, in this colorless world, a video showing a youth with long hair and the look of an eighteen-year-old model with a display over his face. The display wasn't the new M2D type, it was the HMD that had been popular a couple of years before. The sepia coloring of the video only served to reinforce that it was in the past. A memory, maybe?

Endrance's memories?

Ryou somehow knew that these were the memories of the player of Endrance. And there was something on the screen in front of the player.

"Mia." The boy called the cat's name.

"My cat. My only friend."

Ryou saw The World on the player's screen. The character model wasn't the current version of The World, rather the previous version. This was two years ago—2015, at least. And even more curious, the interface was inexplicably familiar to Ryou, although he was sure he'd never played the original version. This was Ryou's first experience sharing memories with someone, and it was incredibly strange.

The player's character was the one that he had used in the previous version of the game, before Endrance, a quiet-looking Wavemaster, a class that no longer existed.

And in front of the boy was a cat. It was clearly based on a cat, and it had fur all over, but a woman's body. A catgirl, so to speak. It must have been an illegal build, as beast hybrids were not an option in the original game.

The Wavemaster and the cat seemed to be a couple, that much was clear.

In a second, the movie flicked to seeing the cat character held up by an invisible power, and crying out in agony. It looked like a sacrifice on an altar.

The crying turned into a scream as the character was ripped apart at the torso, and entrails of data were extracted in the search for an important item hidden inside the character . . . and out it came, a Factor. It looked like a jewel, shining deep crimson, and it was removed as if by the hand of a god.

"They killed her!" Endrance's player howled in agony. It was not a voice, but felt more like words burned in blood red on a white background. Grief. Despair. Hatred. All these human vices became words and burned themselves into Haseo's brain.

The remains of Mia after the extraction were dumped in front of the Wavemaster. The PC resembled a cat that had been hit by a car in the middle of the road.

"They killed my Mia!"

It was so sudden. And he didn't understand why it had happened. A single black tear rolled down Endrance's player's face from the HMD.

And Haseo understood: This Wavemaster was the same player now behind Endrance.

"What is this?"

"These are Endrance's player's memories."

Someone new appeared in the white space. He was far away and up high, his position corresponding to the commentator's seat in the Arena. It was Ovan.

"Ovan."

"So, the contact between two Avatars brought the player's memories into The World as if in a movie. . . ."

"The Avatars have that kind of power?" Ryou looked at the player in front of him—Endrance's player, years ago.

"It's not as much a power as a phenomenon," Ovan said. "You could call it an Avatar Space, a place where online and offline, past and present, player and player all come together . . . where something new begins to exist."

"An Avatar Space . . ."

"AIDA affix themselves to the human mind," Ovan explained. "Much like a narcotic. They show you what you want to see. They make you dependent on them. And then, in the end, they take away everything."

"Ovan . . . ?"

"Look deeply at Endrance, Haseo. . . ."

● ⬡ ●

Color flooded back into the white space. The roar of the arena brought Ryou back to himself.

Haseo and Endrance stood upon the battlefield.

"Not dead . . . will be with Mia forever. . . ." Endrance moved his mouth dryly, his expression blank.

Endrance's consciousness was with the thoughts of the past that Ryou had glimpsed, bound by his memory of loss. He was not living in the present at all, but had chosen to reject what was going on around him and to reside in the past.

Haseo stared across at his opponent. He had to figure him out.

Ovan had told him: Know what your opponent is. Know who you may one day fight. Never get carried away by your emotions. Never let yourself be led by your opponent. Know what it is you must do to fulfill your objective.

He looked at the cat on Endrance's shoulder. The cat, alertly discerning his gaze, raised its hackles and hissed menacingly.

The cat was alive. It was a living entity within The World, too vividly alive for the 'net.

"Endrance," Haseo understood it, "the AIDA that's infecting you . . ."

"You looked into my heart!" Endrance screamed. He'd tried to block out all the voices from outside, everything that would intrude into his memory.

Haseo drew Skeith, unflinching. The cat screeched. The Avatar's scythe blade struck a glancing blow at the cat, and black foam streamed forth—the black spots of an AIDA.

"You snuck into a crack in Endrance's heart, masquerading as his dead cat."

The cat's form was dissolving, its black foam adhering to Endrance's shoulder and eating into its host. It became . . . an indescribable creature, growing into an AIDA monster in the debased form of a man.

"AAAAAAAAAAHHHH!" Endrance grieved, heartbroken at the loss of the false cat that had filled the emptiness in his soul. His hollow heart having lost that which shaped it, it could no longer support him, and he deflated as though a balloon.

"The cat is dead," Haseo laughed cynically. He cared not in the least about the circumstances, or in the images of the death of the catgirl from before. *So what?* he thought. "Pathetic."

Ryou swore, swore upon Haseo's existence: "I will never give up on Shino . . . on my fight!" A person's life depended on it.

"Yes, Haseo! An Avatar's power depends on your strength of mind," Ovan's voice reverberated. "If you're committed . . . having someone you must save makes a man stronger!"

Haseo spoke. "You try saying that again!" He drew the great scythe.

"AAAAAAAHH!" The AIDA monster that had implanted in Endrance was attacking.

"Do I have to spell it out for you, Endrance?"

Together with the murderous blade, its crescent moon the very image of Death, Ryou and Haseo became one. Skeith flashed down upon the AIDA. "You have no power!"

Endrance lay defeated on the ground. Beyond his outstretched fingers, the body of the cat lay stretched out upon the earth. At some length, he comprehended its presence. "Mia . . ."

Suddenly, upon the cat's forehead, a mark as if it had been shot with a gun appeared, and grew with the passing moments until it consumed half the cat's face. Further holes appeared spotted all across, devouring the cat's body as though it were being moth-eaten.

"Nooooooooo!" As if pouring from an egg with a broken shell, Endrance vented his ragged emotions upon the battlefield. In no time at all, the cat's body had been eaten by holes, and the holes themselves vanished into thin air.

An AIDA had impersonated Endrance's cat. . . .

Ryou hadn't had any way of knowing the past of Endrance's player or of Mia. But he'd understood the AIDA manifestation before him and eliminated it. That was enough.

Over the top of the thunderous cheering, the commentating GM was saying something. This reverberating fanfare was to celebrate the crowning of a new champion.

"Heh."

Through his tiredness, Ryou forced a smile. The spectators had seen nothing, neither the Avatar nor Endrance's memories. They had seen only that Haseo had appeared to finish Endrance off in a single blow.

He looked up at the multivision screen and the commentator's seat. But there was no sign of Ovan.

"Hmm? Is it over?" In the spectator seating, Gabi from Kestrel was pounding the shoulder of a nearby PC.

"He won." Pi raised a hand to the bridge of her glasses, as if thinking upon something.

"It seems Haseo's will exceeded even my imagination," Kuhn sighed.

"No way . . . there's just no way . . ." Sakubo—Saku—looked on in shock at Endrance laying prone upon the battlefield. "You'll regret this, Haseo!"

"That was interesting data." And so, to analyze the intriguing data he had collected, Yata turned again to the Serpent of Lore.

As for Ovan . . .

CHAPTER_06: THE ROYAL ISLAND

ONE

All who know Mac Anu know that it is nestled in the center of a great lagoon. Few know of the island visible from the port in the south of the city. And even fewer know its name: the Isle of Kings, Hy Brasail.

The isle is inaccessible by foot, and no Chaos Gate will take you there. There is only one time when players may walk the Isle, and that is to celebrate the crowning of a new Arena Emperor.

And on this day, the isle was flooded. Millions of players had come to see Haseo claim his prize and join in the festivities.

"What has The World witnessed today?" boomed the Game Master from his pedestal. "Whose names are carried on by the river of time for all eternity? Legends, that's who!"

The crowd remained stony silent. But this didn't deter the GM. "The victors are men above men! They know the true meaning of power! And today, a new legend is born! Everyone, give a warm welcome to . . . Emperor Haseo!"

Another spotlight appeared directly over Haseo, and the crowd went wild, all screaming at once in an ear-splitting hubbub.

But they didn't know anything. None of them knew what had really happened. Haseo had beaten Endrance. And in doing so, he had taken down a great AIDA. Ryou had proven to himself that he had the power he needed to take out Tri-Edge and to bring Shino back.

Nobody else could wield, or even understand, that power. Nobody else could bring Shino back, Haseo was sure of it. It could be only him. And that was what kept him going. He understood it all now. He had emerged victorious. And he was loving every second of it.

The GM began to explain about the event item Haseo had won—an item that any player would give an arm and a leg to own, but one that meant nothing to Ryou. He didn't care about any wonderful rare items, or his guaranteed entry into the prestigious Icolo Guild. All he needed was his Avatar.

"And now our ceremony draws to an end!" the GM announced. "Ladies and gentlemen, please enjoy the party and get to know your fellow players!"

Haseo stepped down from the platform and joined the party. There were some faces he knew, and a lot that he didn't. Gabi from Kestrel, Sakaki from Moon Tree . . . they would stand out anywhere. But Haseo couldn't care less about the two great opposing guilds, their Guild Masters, or their members. He had surpassed the system, and yet all that the rest of the players saw was a low-level Multi-Weapon. He was no longer a simple level 133 character. Now he was a demon with a great and illegal power, one that he would never lose or give up.

"Ha-Haseo?" The small voice came from an equally small Warlock, who Haseo identified as Sakubo.

"Hmm? Oh! Bo, right? I guess there's no chance Saku'd come to celebrate me beating her precious Master En."

"Haseo, I-I want to say thanks."

"What? Why?"

"I didn't get the chance to before, when you saved me from that Bordeaux woman."

"Oh, right. Nah, that was nothing." Haseo grinned. "Hey, have you seen anyone else we know?"

"Um, I was with Kuhn a couple of minutes ago, but then he disappeared. . . ."

And just as Bo said that, Haseo spotted Kuhn passing by with a horde of girls clinging to him. Haseo couldn't help but smirk. Only Kuhn would use a sacred ceremony to hit on girls.

"And, um, Atoli said she was coming," Bo said.

Haseo immediately began looking around the crowd for her, but then quickly berated himself.

What am I doing? Not like I care whether she's here or not. I don't need to bother myself with that child anymore.

Haseo quit crowd-scanning and decided it was time for him to take off to somewhere less rowdy.

● ◆ ●

Meanwhile, Atoli was over on another part of the isle, thinking about Haseo. She couldn't go and greet him, not after how they'd parted before. She hadn't even been able to watch the ceremony.

"Are you sure you don't want to congratulate him?"

Atoli jumped violently at the sudden interruption and looked around to see where the voice was coming from—a man with colored glasses standing by the terrace entrance.

"Oh . . . you were the commentator for Haseo's title match, right?" asked Atoli.

Ovan offered a small nod in reply and came over to stand by her. "I'm sure Haseo is wondering where you are, don't you agree?"

"Of course not. Haseo doesn't care about me," Atoli said sadly.

"Did you two have a fight?" Ovan asked in a concerned voice.

Atoli thought for a second. "No, not a fight . . . I think he just hates me. I'm dumb and silly, and I just keep making him mad at me."

"Dumb?" Ovan let out a small laugh. "Haseo isn't exactly a shining example of cleverness himself."

"What do you mean?" asked Atoli, puzzled.

"It doesn't matter. But you want to be close to him, don't you?"

Atoli blushed furiously but answered honestly. "Yes."

"Well then," Ovan continued as if revealing a great secret, "that might not be as impossible as you think."

"What should I do?" Atoli asked.

Ovan looked at her, at her determined face, and smiled. "Excellent question." He leaned over and began to whisper ominously in her ear.

"Ovan?!" It was then that Haseo showed up.

"Haseo," Atoli said in her usual meek tones.

Ryou looked from Atoli's panicked face to Ovan. What the hell was he doing here? And why was Atoli with him?

"Why the hell are you here?!" Haseo said to them with venom in his voice.

"Now now, Haseo, she has every right to be here. It's a free World. Aren't you always saying that?" Ovan said lightly, infuriating Haseo. Why was he defending her?

"Now don't be so hostile. We're old friends, aren't we?" Ovan remained calm under Haseo's furious glare.

"We're only old friends because you've been off doing whatever the hell you do and telling me to go wherever you want me to!" Ryou shouted, infuriated at Ovan's matter-of-fact tone.

Ovan ignored Haseo's yelling and looked from Atoli to Haseo, and then from Haseo to Atoli. He smiled. "Well, well, this brings back memories now, doesn't it?"

Ryou froze as he took in what Ovan meant. Atoli just stared at them, confused.

"Reminds you of the good times, doesn't it?"

Ryou balked. "Atoli has nothing to do with Twilight Brigade!"

"Wandering from dungeon to dungeon, town to town, searching for a certain something. We never did find it, but we had the best of times. You, me, and Shino . . . Twilight Brigade. Seeing the three of us here really brings me back."

"Shut up," Haseo growled.

"Um . . . sorry, but what's this about Twilight Brigade and . . . Shino?" Atoli was understandably confused.

"What? He didn't tell you anything about it?" Ovan said in mock surprise.

"Shut up." Haseo said, growling louder.

Ovan ignored him and continued.

"Before he became a PKK, Haseo was a member of my guild, Twilight Brigade."

"Oh, I remember you saying something about that during the title match," said Atoli.

"Twilight Brigade was set up to find a certain something hidden in The World," Ovan went on.

"Something?" Atoli asked. "A treasure-hunting guild?"

"Not exactly. Have you ever heard the legend of the Key of the Twilight?"

"No, I haven't."

"It is the ultimate item. The legends say that it is the key to making all your wishes come true in The World. It's obviously not listed in any guide books for the game."

"But why would you want to find something like that?" Atoli asked, still not following. "And this Shino . . . was a member of the guild?"

"Yes. She was a member of Twilight Brigade. But she—"

"Ovan!" Haseo broke in furiously, but Ovan continued to ignore him.

"One day about six months ago, Shino was PKed while playing The World. And since then, she hasn't logged in once. Nobody has heard a word from her."

"Because she was PKed?" Atoli asked. "Did she quit the game?"

Haseo was fuming too much to explain about the coma, so he let Ovan go on.

"Shino and Haseo were very close," Ovan said gently. "They had even kept in contact in the real world. I think they met up . . . did you, Haseo?"

Haseo was shaking now, confusing Atoli even more.

"Atoli, Shino used a PC exactly the same as yours. The exact same."

Atoli was speechless as his words set in. When they met, Haseo had been confused . . . and then angry.

"What the hell is wrong with you?!" Haseo had shouted at her in fury. *"Just get lost, and don't show your face near me ever again!"*

All that, just because their PCs were the exact same. . . .

"That explains everything," Atoli said slowly, an edge to her voice.

Ryou stared. He hadn't expected it to hit him so hard, but it did. "Hey, hold on a second—"

Atoli shouted over him, refusing to accept whatever he had to say. "So this whole time, this *whole time*, you've been comparing me to Shino?!"

"No, I—" Ryou started to protest, but his mouth dried up. Because it was true. He'd been comparing them from the start. He'd just been blowing off steam at Atoli because of Shino.

"You only went adventuring with me because I have the same PC as Shino? You got angry at me because I couldn't do what Shino could? What was I to you, nothing more than a Shino substitute?"

Haseo was speechless. It was all true.

"Haseo, you've been looking down on me this whole time because I'm not who you wanted me to be!" With that, Atoli turned and fled from the terrace in tears.

Haseo couldn't follow her. He had sworn that she was nothing to him, that he never wanted to see her again. And now he didn't know what to do. He was upset and miserable, and was already regretting every single thing he'd done to her.

"You're quite the slave to duty, Haseo," Ovan said.

"Ovan . . ." Haseo managed to say.

"You've spent these six months torturing yourself for losing Shino. You can't just tell the people around you to go away." It was like a teacher telling off his top student for being the class joker. The irony and shame of it all burned deep within Ryou.

"So this is where you were, Haseo?" It was the GM, who appeared seemingly out of nowhere on the terrace. "We can't very well have a party without the guest of honor! What have you been doing here all by yourself?"

"By myself?" Haseo whirled around, but Ovan had disappeared. Yet again, he'd appeared, said his piece, and left.

Ovan . . . what is it that you really want?

Of course, the Key of the Twilight. But why was he weaving such a big web of plans for it? And what role did Ryou have to play in this grand scheme?

Atoli . . .

The pain he'd caused the poor girl was finally sinking in completely now, and it hurt him more than he could have imagined.

The GM's voice interrupted Haseo's thoughts. "Right, back to the party we go."

"What? Oh . . . right." Haseo moved to follow the GM away from the terrace.

●⬡●

The party went on. And Ryou, who should have been over the moon, felt more like he was at the bottom of the ocean. He had his Avatar, his power. He held the coveted position of arena champion. But it was all empty now.

"Now there's a face that could cancel Christmas."

Haseo looked up. "Oh, Kuhn."

"Just got dumped, huh?"

"What?" Haseo stared at him.

"Bull's-eye," Kuhn said, satisfied.

"Can it. I'm not like you," Haseo responded gruffly.

There were no girls after Kuhn anymore. It seemed that his pickup lines hadn't had much of a lasting effect. But then, what could you possibly expect from trying to pick up girls online?

"Anyway, listen."

Haseo responded to Kuhn with blank silence. But when Kuhn answered back with a serious face and mentioned Epitaph Users, Haseo was all ears.

"We need to talk. It's about Atoli."

"What about her?"

Kuhn didn't answer. And before Haseo could press further, his screen went black.

The next thing Haseo saw on his screen was not the Isle of Kings, but the Gate of Uroboros. Kuhn was standing beside him, silently looking ahead. Haseo followed his line of sight and saw . . . Pi, the Tribal Grappler, and Yata, the Macabre Dancer.

"Raven?!"

He was in front of the illegal Serpent of Lore, in the back of Raven's @Home.

Pi took a step forward and gave Haseo an appraising glance. "Nice work, Kuhn."

"No prob."

Haseo was caught completely off guard. "Kuhn? What the hell?"

"Kuhn is a member of Raven, Haseo," Pi informed him, leaving Ryou dumbfounded.

"I never said I wasn't, Haseo—but you never asked," Kuhn explained in his usual cheery way as he walked over toward Pi, the image of innocence.

"So you're one of them?" Haseo turned to glare at Yata. "What the hell is going on here? Having a setup like this, kidnapping players … What are you, hackers?"

It was hardly an unfair question. Everyone knew that there were hackers in The World, whose favorite pastime was messing around with the game. Maybe Raven was a group of those, too.

"Don't be silly," Pi told him, adjusting her glasses. "We work for CC Corp, the creators of The World."

"You what?" Haseo's voice faltered. They weren't players, they were CC Corp employees. The sudden revelation was hard to believe—but if they were admins, that would explain how they'd been able to follow his every move. And they could've found out who he was from his login information. With a worldwide conglomerate like CC Corp, privacy wasn't even an issue.

"So this area's a Game Master's den?" Haseo had read about such places in articles about the game.

"No. We're not GMs, though you can call us that if you want," Pi answered. So she wasn't a user-support GM, anyway.

"Then what are you?" Haseo asked.

"Raven is merely a front," Pi said. "We are CC Corp's Team G.U., the anti-AIDA team."

"G.U. . . ." The letters didn't mean anything to Haseo. He ran the letters through The World's terminology database, but nothing came up. He was clearly knee deep in something that went far past the normal running of The World.

"G.U.?" Suddenly, the initials appeared in the database, though it had clearly shown no results before. His database had been updated, but by whom?

"Project G.U.," Yata spoke up. "And you, Haseo, you are a very important element of Project G.U."

"What?"

"Ryou Misaki, like it or not, you are a very important research subject for us."

The Serpent of Lore then showed a hologram of a certain wounded character.

"Shino!" It was Shino's grayed-out body.

"Haseo, now you will join us." Yata wasn't asking. It was an order

"Sorry, no chance," Haseo shot back, giving Yata a glare.

"Excuse me?"

"Like I'd trust CC Corp after you've been hiding Shino away and covering up everything that's been happening!" Haseo turned and made to walk away.

"I wonder, are you really any better?" Pi mused.

A window popped up in front of Haseo. It showed a young man laying on a hospital bed. And the face . . . Haseo recognized it instantly. It was the same face he'd seen back at the Arena.

"That can't be . . . Endrance?"

"Endrance's player has fallen into a coma," Pi told him. "Most likely right after he fought you. You turned someone else into a Lost One. That doesn't make you much different than Tri-Edge, does it?"

Any retort Ryou had died in his throat. He had done this to Endrance. He had turned a real person comatose by attacking him online. The reality of what he had done hit him like a hammer.

"From the standpoint of the system administrators, and from the standpoint of G.U., you must be kept restrained."

"And Endrance?" Haseo asked.

"Nobody knows how to save him. Just like Shino Nanao," Pi replied brusquely.

Kuhn spoke up in a diplomatic tone. "Will you work with us? With G.U.? The power of your Avatar can be used to combat the AIDA menace and help save every other player out there."

Haseo, still reeling from the shock of what he'd done to Endrance, took his time to reply. When he did, it was only a brash outburst that sounded false even to him.

"So what do you want?"

"You are worried about Atoli, are you not?" Yata said, as if he had read Haseo's mind.

"Atoli . . ."

"We are also investigating Atoli."

"What? Why?"

"We believe that she may be another Epitaph User."

"What?!" So even Atoli could call forth an Avatar . . . even she had that power.

"We only discovered this recently. A few days ago, in fact, when she joined up with you and you discovered Tri-Edge's sign. We believe she may have the ability to hear AIDA."

"Why didn't you say anything?!"

"All you wanted was information on Tri-Edge. And on your own Avatar. I believe you were quite clear in saying that was all you were interested in."

"Dammit."

The console in front of Yata lit up, and as if in response, the Serpent of Lore began to activate. An information window popped up, showing Haseo facing Endrance in the Demon Palace tournament . . . and Atoli watching the battle.

"She came to see?" Haseo stared.

The video fast-forwarded to the ceremony. It was clear that Yata had been keeping his eye on Atoli the entire time. Currently in the video, she was up on the terrace talking to Ovan.

"You know the three-pronged mark that Haseo's been searching for?"

"Yes . . ."

"He's looking for the one who made that mark, Tri-Edge. And you can help him, with your audio ability."

"My audio ability?"

"If you can do what Shino couldn't, then Haseo will be sure to appreciate you."

Atoli had asked about Shino, then run away toward the wharf on the Isle of Kings. From there to the port of Mac Anu, and from there . . .

"The Chaos Gate?" Atoli was running at top speed toward the Chaos Gate, and then she transferred.

"That is all we have," Yata said.

"What? How?"

"The Serpent of Lore cannot trace Atoli to the area she transferred to following the ceremony. It's as if she simply disappeared."

"But you work for the system! How can you just lose someone?" It wasn't making any sense.

"She hasn't logged out, but we still can't find her."

"How——?"

"She is Lost, not within the regular system." Yata's words had a dark undertone.

AIDA . . .

"Where did she go? The keywords?" Haseo asked.

"Delta Hidden Forbidden Bulwark."

"A Lost Ground?"

"Yes. Morrigu Barrow. I believe you discovered it some time ago as part of Twilight Brigade."

"Dammit," Haseo said angrily. "Dammit, Atoli!"

"Kuhn and I will accompany you," Pi informed him. And before Haseo knew it, the three of them were in a party together. He was definitely dealing with admins here.

"My first time being in a full party of Epitaph Users," Kuhn mused, implying that Pi was an Epitaph User, too.

"I'm sending you to Morrigu Barrow now. Delta Hidden Forbidden Bulwark . . ." Yata's words faded away as Haseo began the transfer.

● ⬡ ●

TWO

△ HIDDEN FORBIDDEN BULWARK MORRIGU BARROW WALL

A small grassy plain overshadowed by an endless castle wall—Morrigu Barrow Wall. It was said that it marked the barrier between this world and the next.

Haseo, Kun, and Pi materialized together, and the first thing to catch their eye was a mark carved into the wall in front of them.

"Tri-Edge's sign . . ." Ryou couldn't believe what he was seeing. The sign was still glowing red.

"Looks like the mark's still pretty new," Kuhn observed.

"This sign definitely wasn't here when the Brigade found this place," Haseo said.

"This must be connected to Atoli's disappearance." Pi began to examine the mark carefully.

"Let me." Haseo targeted the sign. Last time he'd encountered this sign, while traveling with Atoli and Sakubo, it had transferred them to the underground lake at Indieglut Lugh. And that was where they'd encountered Endrance and that cat AIDA he'd been keeping.

Morrigu Barrow, the wall between this life and the next. And the mark was a chink in the wall, or possibly even a gateway.

Haseo laid his hand on it and selected it, and then his screen went black.

It wasn't just the screen. It felt like his entire being was floating, terrified, through the barrier, sinking into the darkness. It was like taking the vertical drop of a rollercoaster, except that this one wasn't ending.

When his feet finally touched the ground, he let out a sigh of relief.

An online game shouldn't be able to do this to me. . . .

White. Everywhere he looked, the screen was white.

"Where are we?" Pi glanced around.

"I thought we were never going to land," Kuhn said, and Haseo thanked his lucky stars that at least one other person there wasn't cold and calculating.

Looking around they saw, of all things, a row of coin lockers. And in front of them was a single Harvest Cleric, Atoli, panting as she tried to force open one of the lower lockers.

"Atoli . . ." Haseo had a cautionary tone in his voice as he moved toward the PC.

"Haseo? What are you doing here?" Atoli turned around, still squatting.

"I should ask you the same thing. What are you doing?"

"Keep back!" The urgency in Atoli's voice made Haseo freeze in his tracks. "I found this place with my own special ability! So stay back and let me use that ability to find Tri-Edge!"

"Atoli, what do you want with Tri-Edge?"

"I told you!" Atoli was getting hysterical now, and Haseo could practically hear the player behind her. "It's because I want you to accept me—not as Shino, but as me!"

"That's what you wanted? *That?*" Ryou didn't understand her. Why would Atoli go that far to help someone else? It didn't make any sense.

"Shino is Shino. And you're Atoli." It was such an obvious thing to say, but it was all he could think of. He imagined it would do the job. They were different people, after all.

"No, no!" Atoli shook her head wildly. "If there's another, stronger Harvest Cleric, you'll pick her! If there's someone kinder, like Shino, you'll trust her! Or if not Shino, whomever's stronger, not me!"

"Atoli . . ." Haseo was speechless again. Atoli was getting good at picking out his faults lately.

"I don't want to always be in second or third or whatever place! I want people to care about *me!* Nobody cares a thing about me in the real world! They won't even look at me!" It wasn't Haseo she had the problem with; it was herself.

"What the hell? You need to stop worrying about what other people think of you and start working on how you think of yourself!" Haseo shouted, and Atoli shrank back.

Ryou thought better of shouting, and instead opted for a calmer voice. "The truth is, when I first saw you, I was reminded of Shino. And when you acted so silly, I took that as an insult to Shino."

"I knew it," Atoli said sadly.

"But that's different now." Ryou was opening up his heart to Atoli—and, for the first time, to himself. "I'd just gone back to level 1, and I was insecure and raging. But you didn't look down on me, not once. Neither did Sakubo. You both supported me. We went to dungeons together, traveled together. . . . I don't know if I can truly believe in you or not, but when I'm with you . . . I feel comfortable."

"Haseo . . ."

"It's the first time I've felt that way after losing Shino and restarting The World. I was trying to be strong, so I acted up on you and hurt you. And if it weren't for you . . . I might not be here. Maybe the PKs would have caught me, maybe something else. But the reason I came here was to find you."

"Really?"

"I'm not really good at saying these kinds of things, but I don't lie. I swear."

Atoli slowly stood up. "Then I . . ."

But she was cut off. An irregularity suddenly drew everyone's attention. Blue wave patterns appeared in the air, revealing . . .

"Tri-Edge." Haseo would recognize those twin blades and that cadaverous body anywhere. "You . . ."

"That's him?" Pi and Kuhn readied themselves.

Haseo lost himself completely, overcome with hatred for the creature that had taken Shino from him, humiliated him—and brought out his ultimate weapon, his Avatar . . . his anti-AIDA weapon.

"So what the hell are you, anyway?" Haseo challenged Tri-Edge. "A cheater? An Epitaph User? An AIDA-PC? Why the hell have you been putting people into comas?!"

"Lost Ones? Comas? What's going on?" Atoli asked, completely confused.

Tri-Edge gave no reply and silently drew his three-pronged blades. Ryou responded by targeting him. The name that came up on the screen was Azure Kite.

"What the hell?" But Haseo wasn't planning on being caught off guard again. Now he had his new power, drawn forth from the hole in his heart.

"I am . . . the Terror of Death!"

His Avatar took its shape, a crescent-moon scythe. "Skeith!"

He gripped the handle of the scythe and bore down on Azure Kite.

"The Propagation . . . Magus!"

"The Avenger . . . Tarvos!"

Kuhn and Pi both called their own Avatars forth. A long spear made up of green crystals. Knuckles with spikes like beasts' claws. These were the only weapons effective against the illegal AIDA.

"How do I bring the Lost Ones back?!" Haseo beat at Azure Kite. "Answer me!"

Haseo's Data Drain hit Azure Kite straight on, and it fell to its knees. The data making up its body began to crumble.

"Was that it?"

"I must finish this!" Pi flew at Azure Kite with Tarvos and punched right through him.

"Wait!" Haseo shouted. "He has to tell us how to return the Lost Ones!"

But it was too late. Pi's attack shattered Azure Kite's patchwork body into pieces, which became fragments, and then grains, and finally disappeared.

"What . . . happened?" Atoli was baffled.

"Atoli?"

"Haseo, what were those weapons? And that ability?"

Kuhn broke in. "Atoli, you can see Avatars?"

But just as he was about to tell Atoli everything, the doors of the coin lockers began to fly open. Haseo could see shapes inside, like masses of bees swarming.

"Atoli! Get away from there!" he shouted.

"Huh?"

As the last door opened, the shapes all flew out and surrounded Atoli. Black arms, black hands, one for each door. They grabbed her arms, her legs, her head . . . and dragged her toward the coin lockers.

All that was left of Atoli was a high-pitched scream.

The coin locker doors all closed at once, trapping Atoli on the other side. And Haseo's resulting scream echoed out into the endless white.

"ATOLI!"

AFTERWORD

G.U. is part of the .hack project and is a series of manga, anime, and novels based on the Bandai-Namco games.

This book is not a straight novelization of the game.

I went back to the original storyboards for the basic story of this novel.

In other words, just like the people at CyberConnect2 used those image boards and characters to create a story suitable for a video game, I used those same boards as the basis for a written story. I wrote something that would suit a light novel format using the basic images and creations.

I feel that the games and novels both came from the original source. Neither is correct or incorrect.

The World has many forms.

Within The World are a great number of stories.

The characters live on.

For the creators of G.U., we wanted to make it so that the story was loose, so that everyone could enjoy it differently. I hope we achieved that.

I hope to see you again in the next volume.

Haseo has his Avatar. Now the story of G.U. can move on to Haseo fighting against the game system.

— Tatsuya Hamazaki, March 2007